TO AN ANGEL WHO IS NEW

TO AN ANGEL WHO IS NEW

Arno Bohlmeijer

William B. Eerdmans Publishing Company

Grand Rapids, Michigan / Cambridge, U.K.

Wm. B. Eerdmans Publishing Co.
255 Jefferson Ave. S.E., Grand Rapids, Michigan 49503 /
P.O. Box 163, Cambridge CB3 9PU U.K.

Printed in the United States of America

08 07 06 05 04   5 4 3 2 1

Library of Congress Cataloging-in-Publication Data

Bohlmeijer, Arno.
[Aan een engel die nieuw is. English]
To an angel who is new / Arno Bohlmeijer.
p.   cm.
ISBN 0-8028-1032-2 (pbk.: alk. paper)
I. Title.

PT5881.12.O365A62513   2004
839.31'364 — dc22

2004040901

www.eerdmans.com

TO AN ANGEL WHO IS NEW

In the middle of conflict and confusion, heaven came so close to earth that I wanted to show how and share it.

The heroine of my life was Marian, but I won't tell much about the past. I wouldn't know where to start, and after this drastic turning point, I don't want to look back too much, certainly not at *me*. Readers will get to know us as we go along, beyond death.

After writing a chapter or two, I found it was painful and strange to mention Marian in the third person, making her distant. I could not continue unless I addressed her directly.

Consequently, I don't "introduce" some of the people in this account, since Marian knows them! But then, it makes no difference if they are relatives, friends, neighbors, or colleagues; what matters is that they've come to help. Readers may take them for granted or be as grateful to them as I am.

So I have begun afresh — in words as well as in life.

There . . . and here,
where your voice was,
goes the breath of wind.
It seems to speak for you
but hushes in the light,
that stays and is free.

November-December

You've desperately been trying to involve me in the care of our children. The problem is not the amount of time I spend with them but the *quality* of the attention I give them. What you mean by that and to what extent I've failed as a father for years dawns on me awkwardly, slowly, and whether I'll be able to change . . .

In these attempts to reach me — before it's too late — you seem to be driven: strained to the limit, as if you have a goal with a deadline.

Yet, we can laugh about the irony of life when an editor says about the manuscript of a new book, "Good, but the family in this story is a bit too harmonious." And, shamefaced, I read a review of the previous one: "Bohlmeijer seems to have a sixth sense for what's going on in children's minds."

Early one morning, I dream vividly that we're in the car, driving at full speed, and I'm at the wheel. We hit some kind of curb; something is happening that belongs to the world of television; the wheel slips out of my hands. Somebody cries, "What are you doing?" and "Watch out!" But there's nothing I *can* do now. We crash into something big and hard.

I wake up trembling. The dream was so physically real that I stay shaken all day. I've never had a foretelling dream before, and I'm not afraid, but the blow from it remains in my body. I keep this to myself.

To a friend, you say, "I'm ready for a very, very new phase," and, strangely, "All that's left for me to do is lie down and rest. From now on, it's truly up to Arno."

⚬⚬⚬

Sunday, December 13th

Discussing Leon's birthday gathering, I must have said it: You're exhausted. At first, we don't seem to be going at all, because I'm still feverish myself, after the flu, and you should really stay home for a precious afternoon of quiet — or should I say, for a last chance to keep up with life. But you decide to join us — so sweet — and it's striking how sincerely you *want* to.

We take our time getting ready, showering and washing our hair and choosing warm, comfortable clothes. Sometimes we wear easy jeans-and-sweaters for weeks; other times we enjoy putting on a festive, flattering outfit or something we're attached to.

I love the subtle, daring way you combine colors, al-

8

ways producing new accessories and managing to be elegant and casual at the same time. Each detail remains inconspicuous, but your appearance is a caress.

For the first time I'm wearing my Peruvian wool sweater, which is so warm that it's sat on the shelf for over a year. Which can't be! What a way to discover how time can vanish — for happy or sad reasons. And time can't be blamed; it's totally innocent and always fair, just being its frank self. That's why we often run fast or slow.

Rosemyn says we look nice. Sucking her thumb, she leans against the warmth of my sweater.

As usual, I'm the one who's driving. You drive very well, scrupulously, *not* fifty-one where fifty is the limit, and not passing unless it's more than safe, which tends to annoy me when I'm the passenger. I never do anything unsafe, have never caused an accident, but I drive fifty-five on the roads we know well, evoking your anger and fear.

"Be careful," you always say when I leave on my own, and it's never become a mere habit. I always reassure you, pleased with your caring, which is true and profound at moments that can easily become routine.

In Wornfield, the traffic situation has been changed considerably: narrowed lanes, new islands, speed limit reduced to thirty-five — rightly so for the people who live there.

I don't adjust on time and just touch a curb. "Well, this is mighty radical."

"I hit one last week," you say. "Luckily, I was driving slowly."

"It's like a bobsleigh run!"

I think we're relieved now, because we've *both* made "the mistake."

Arriving at Lauren and John's, I'm thinking, *They should come out and see how their old Volvo has been restored.* But this isn't the right time for that. I'd better not stay out in the cold myself.

It's a quiet, cozy family party. As the "little one" of six, Phoebe keeps running after the kittens, even when they escape into the garage. They make her blissfully happy, and I can't think of anything more beautiful than watching her hugging them.

But we leave early. It's nearly her bedtime, anyway.

I hate slow good-byes; I sit and wait for you in the car. You're chatting with Lauren for so long that I have enough time to admonish myself: *Calm down. It's a good exercise in patience, fair enough, and the children don't seem to have a problem with it. . . .*

Lauren is the last to talk with you — or at least, hers are the last words to be remembered for now. And without any of us knowing it, they're about the day you will die. "Would you like to come and spend Christmas here?"

Lauren thinks you're transparently tired, silent, withdrawn, but not in a negative way. She has good, kind eyes. I mean: She can see with her soul.

Next, I know vaguely that we're off. Whether I grumbled or we talked about little or special things, I can't remember. Nor what Rosemyn and Phoebe said or did. I don't recall anything, although we still were on our way together, lived a life together, for ten more minutes.

We're beside each other, the gearbox in between us, and I suppose we're just looking in front of us, on the road in the dark.

I've been told this by many: Just outside Wornfield, I hit a traffic island in a bend, and because I'm trying to regain control of the car or am losing control completely, we run off the road, head on into a strong tree. There's only one big tree there in the fields.

Eyewitnesses call 911.

At this very moment a police car comes from the opposite direction. It stops and a woman called Ina gets out. Through a broken window in our car she talks to Rosemyn, the only one of us who's not unconscious — a nine-year-old girl with very big eyes. Ambulances, more police cars, and fire engines arrive. A boy in Rosemyn's class has heard the sirens.

Her foot is stuck; the back seat is jammed forward. She doesn't cry or scream, only says her arm hurts and asks a few times, "Has this really happened?"

She doesn't ask for you or me. What a mercy there's someone who helps her.

A window is removed; a firefighter pulls Rosemyn out of the wreck and takes her onto his lap. He has two little girls himself.

"Not to the hospital," she keeps saying. And, "I don't want a shot."

You are pressed against the underside of the dashboard. Ina is worried by the sounds you make, indicating serious internal injuries.

Both of Phoebe's feet are stuck. She's fallen between our seats, and her head is on your shoulder at a strange angle. When Ina puts it right, Phe vomits.

Somebody who works for John happens to be cycling by on his way home. He recognizes the white Volvo and calls Lauren and John, so they and my parents are informed very early.

I am lying in the field. My door was thrust open by the blow of impact, and I was thrown out of the car — I wasn't wearing a seat belt. Which probably saved my life, according to the police.

The fact that the children are alive is a miracle too: any car without this thick steel of 1966 would have been completely demolished. And it's *you* who made the choice between restoring the Volvo and switching to an "ordinary" secondhand car. The dilemma was on our minds for weeks; it was about safety, money, and even emotional attachment. One afternoon, driving home from work, I could finally make a decision (time was short): Let's take the VW that seemed to fall into our laps. But when I got home, you were on the phone, saying, "Let Pete come and work on the Volvo when he's ready."

While the children are put on stretchers and Phe's given an IV drip on the spot, Dad and John arrive and give the police all the necessary information, so they won't need to question Rosemyn.

Two ambulances leave for Denton, with you and

Rosemyn, and two for Southmere, with Phe and me. How this was decided I don't know, but it was farsighted judgment.

When the paramedic tries to talk to Rosemyn, it only works in snatches, because most of the time she's in her shell. "Blood on the floor," she says a few times. Then, again and again, "Don't talk about it. So horrible . . ." And when he gives her an injection: "It was hurting already. . . ."

My mam tells Lauren about a dream she had about ten days ago (when I had mine too): "I was in a cemetery, near an open grave. People were passing by two by two. I didn't see their faces, but one of them asked, 'Who is it?' I said, 'My eldest son. I told him so often: "Drive carefully . . ."'"

In reality, she's never said it but often thought it. What is "reality" now?

The moment she woke up after this dream, she started saving her energy, preparing herself.

Back at Lauren and John's, my dad calls your parents. She only says, "Oh, no . . ." and he, "Who was driving?"

I can understand that this question comes up first. It must be a relief for them to know you didn't cause the accident.

They leave for Denton, where they wait while a whole team of doctors are working on you.

Your brain and abdominal organs are badly injured; a leg and an arm are broken; a heel is crushed.

There's little chance of recovery. They call Judy.

You're under a sheet. Only your head is visible, and fortunately it's not injured. You're still wearing your earrings.

Your mother wants to lift the sheet, but the surgeon won't allow her to. She will only remember how she stroked your face.

My mam and dad go to Southmere Hospital with Lauren and John. Lauren hesitates at first: Should they leave their baffled children behind on Leon's birthday? But John insists, because he realizes how serious the situation is.

Elise and Rachel are crying. Leon is watching sports on television. Later, when they play a game, their laughter is too loud.

Near the site of the crash, the lane is still blocked. The four of them can't but stop and take in the picture; a floodlight shows the wreck and the bustle around it. So, driving to the casualties, not knowing how we are, only that things are bad, they have to join the line of waiting cars, which increases their sense of unrealness.

Phoebe is in Intensive Care, on a life-support system. She has a brain contusion. But her face and the rest of her body are intact.

No visitors are allowed yet; the sub-coma she's in is both her protection and her battle. She has to fight this by herself, on levels of which we have no knowledge.

My lungs have collapsed. They need to be drained, and

for thirty minutes my condition is critical. The fractured upper leg needs surgery: a pin and a bolt will have to be screwed into the bone. Concussion and broken ribs will heal of their own accord.

The four brave ones leave for the hospital in Denton.

In the doorway of your room there, Mam faints and has to wait outside. It's her only "weak" moment; to me it shows the depth of her emotion.

Carefully Lauren touches your shoulder and gives you a kiss. *I realized how lonely she was,* Lauren will tell me one day, *how much I loved her, and I knew she felt my presence.*

She says it out loud now as well: "I love you."

Our families meet in the room where bad news is delivered.

The neurologist comes in and tells them, "The prognosis is 0.0."

You're clinically dead.

When I'm told later that even John cries at this news, it helps make me feel what's happening.

"It must have been the old car," your father says. "I've always hated it. I suppose the brakes were faulty."

John is silent. He more or less *gave* it to us, to keep it in the family.

Dad calls Alex and Ernest. They're both at home, and Phyllis and Nicky are with them, but all four of them were about to leave without their cell phones. A few minutes later, none of them could have been reached.

We're so lucky to have brothers and sisters and in-laws. When they hear the news, they come immediately. We'll never take them for granted again.

Rosemyn has been through half-a-dozen treatments and examinations. A nurse gives her a felt dog. She hasn't cried. There are wounds from shattered glass on her face, mainly around her eyes. For the rest she has "only" a broken arm, and one of the doctors suggests she be taken to Southmere, to be with Phoebe and me. We're stabilized.

When finally the grandparents can see Rosemyn, she's unnaturally cheerful. "Hi! We've crashed! I *told* him: 'Watch out!'"

Of course, she thinks we're going home now — with plasters and bandages — to talk things over theatrically, relieved, and tell all the details to neighbors, friends, and classmates.

Is this strength of character, or are her emotions blocked?

With her arm in a provisional sling, she can be transported in John's car. Sitting between Mam and Lauren in the back, she says, "Drive slowly; we've just had an accident. It's normal to be scared after a crash, isn't it?"

There's also some bravura (one way to cope with the unfathomable?) — ". . . into the curb and . . . bang!" — as well as some exaggeration: "What *I* have is worst, isn't it?" And soon, there's a need for confirmation: "It's Dad's fault. He's the one who crashed."

"But not on purpose. No one does these things on purpose."

So at ten p.m., Rosemyn is going to Southmere. With

her good arm she's resting against Lauren. And why her mam isn't coming . . . Either the question doesn't occur to her yet, or she's afraid to ask it, knowing all too well . . .

Your parents and Judy stay with you, waiting for death. As for me, I can't deal with guilt yet.

Rosemyn's arm is set here, in Southmere Hospital.

"This will hurt a bit."

She doesn't flinch, although she's often yelled about a scratch, hasn't she?

The fracture is too close to the shoulder for either a cast or a bolt and a pin, so Rosemyn's arm has to go in traction. A special bed is fetched for her, and due to the lack of staff (it's Sunday night), John helps to install the complicated gear. He's very good at it; how this would have gone without him . . .

The operation on my leg is finished. John stays with Rosemyn. The others can visit me.

Mam says, "You were unconscious but not 'weak' or shattered. The nurse agreed: you looked strong."

I just *receive* that strength, I can feel it so clearly! We're all witnessing something extraordinary under sublime direction, in the middle of eternity, where earthly horrors will prove to have meaning.

Even more so than sleep, unconsciousness means we're partly in the spiritual world. It protects us from pain and gives us wisdom, free of physical restrictions, perhaps with lasting effects. And that must be true for you more than anyone else.

Rosemyn is taken to a room in the pediatric ward — 6 East. She keeps asking about Phoebe and won't sleep for fear of dreams about the accident. She tells nurse Janet that her seventeen-year-old brother is still at home. Thankfully, her endless imagination can be of some help mentally.

Toward midnight, when her grandparents and aunt and uncle are exhausted and have to go home, she's still awake. There's only one other child in the ward.

Meanwhile, incredibly, you start breathing on your own, so the team of doctors decides to operate after all. Some organs are removed and others repaired; you're given a chance to live.

Maybe it's just as well that I have no say in this; it would be impossible for me to make that choice for you.

Mam and Dad have to make a lot of phone calls to friends and neighbors. They're trying hard to remember names and find numbers. They pick the wrong Jack Henrick in the phone book, leave a message, and are never called back, which we'll soon laugh about.

Cor and Ann are at home, realizing we've never returned with the children this late.

Ann says later, "In the twenty years of our marriage, I've seen Cor cry only twice. The first time, he was overwrought; the second time was after the news of that night."

From now on, crying will be a compliment.

Our neighbors come to the hospital and don't leave until Rosemyn is asleep.

We're asleep when your struggle begins. Why haven't you left yet?

⸙

Monday, December 14th

Rosemyn has had a bad night — she's still frightened — and is pleased with music tapes. Again she asks about Phoebe a few times. Although her face is aching, she refuses Paracetamols. She often rings the nurses' bell, though.

It's Monday, but instead of going to work, Jack shows up at Rosemyn's bedside at eight a.m. He reads to her from a thick book for hours on end.

At the same time, after a night without sleep, Mam finds the phone number of the girls' school and also cancels any of our appointments she happens to know about. Then the trips to both hospitals begin again, and she and Dad drive to our house to get dolls and teddy bears.

So, without conferring, each of many persons fulfills the right task at the right moment.

Jack doesn't leave until Ernest and Nicky take over the reading.

I don't realize there are weekdays on which people go to work — or should have gone.

19

Mam and Dad come to me.

"Press my hand when you hear me," she says.

I press.

But I don't remember. My eyes and throat remain shut. I have no sense of time or space.

They go to Phoebe, who's close by here in the ICU, motionless, and they talk softly to her.

Thanks to a lot of arranging in the background, there's soon a list of people who'd like to help out. Rosemyn will have someone with her continuously.

"Are we going home Saturday?" she keeps asking.

The cuts on her face are dressed. She turns on her side all the time, which is not allowed: the arm should not be moved. But she *has* to move — that's obvious — and tries to ignore the traction altogether, so that an edge of the sling cuts into her skin.

To some people she says, "Dad was making jokes, and he looked over his shoulder, and Mam said to him, 'Never do that again.'"

At this point, nobody tells me about that. Friends have discussed it, but you know how hard it's always been to find out whether Rose is stating facts or making things up — to hide guilt or fears, needing to show them indirectly — and they're not sure I ought to face this problem now.

But you know what happened, don't you?

After the surgery, which takes about eight hours, your condition remains serious. This news is the first memory I have after the accident. I can't see who's brought the information; I can only hear that it's a woman, and her or my insensitivity keeps the meaning of it at a great distance.

The morphine and the breathing machine work well. The moments I come around must be brief and bring no pain, nausea, or discomfort. I don't feel myself, don't know how I'm doing or what I look like. I have no sense of my wounds or the IV drips and tubes in my body. I don't even wonder why I can't speak.

Some emotion comes when Jack stops by my bed in the morning and Lauren is here in the afternoon. Their pain shows me their love so intensely, in these fractions of time, that the past years seem insignificant. They are visiting four casualties, and what we look like can be seen in their eyes and their bearing.

Jack strokes my forearm with his fingertips, an expression of helplessness that helps a great deal.

Lauren bends close to me. I start drawing letters on my chest and watch her concentrating — she's so afraid she won't understand me. Very conscious of her efforts, I want to "write" clearly.

She says each letter: *M-A-R-I-A-N.*

She nods, swallows, and shakes her head. "Not well."

How brave, to look me in the eyes while mustering honesty.

She explains that you don't react, and I know it's a postponed good-bye.

My fault? I ask in the same way.

Her surprise and pity touch me to tears, but I can't cry.

Again she shakes her head, looking for words. Is she aware I don't know *anything* about the accident? Don't know if I failed to yield or ignored red lights. If we collided with anyone else . . .

"No, there was no traffic offense or anything."

Lauren will say about this moment, "I held the hand on your chest and felt the pounding of your heart."

It's her closeness that keeps me whole.

She's going to see you again today — also on my behalf. How glad you'll be of someone's touch. Although it takes some courage, she talks to you out loud, like most of the people who visit you. They've all had moments when the awareness of tubes and machines, of the way you're at their mercy, falls away completely. Then there's an inner contact of sheer beauty — because your soul is almost free from your body?

Lauren says to you, "You've always been brave. . . . Arno and the children are doing well; you can count on that."

Almost everybody feels responses from you, like a motion of your head or a slight swallow or some sort of image they receive inwardly. Begging, loving, or regretting, they ask you to stay, with good intentions for a new start or for a deepening continuation.

"When I'm talking to Marian," one friend says, "I can hear a change in her breathing that's also visible on the monitor."

It strikes another friend that your hair is no longer golden but blonde.

Mam and Dad have been to the police, who think the traffic island I hit is marked insufficiently. The car was in perfect condition, and I drove within the speed limit. Still . . . What if I'd been more alert?

At seven tonight, Jack's here with me again. Among friends and family there's already a web of communication — phone calls until late in the evening — and he's heard that I write on my chest. But now I gesture that I want a pen to write on paper.

I have so little sense of space that Jack has to "steer" the sheet at the right time in the right direction. The words become all mixed up anyway, crooked and wrong. The order will be hard to determine later, and some words really need to be deciphered or disentangled now.

Against tree is a loose end somewhere. Is it my answer to somebody's question, "Do you know what happened?"

Sorry: rabbits.

Is anyone thinking of Pete and Gerry in their hutches? They need water and food twice a day, and we let them stretch their legs in the house or in the run on the lawn.

Of course, four neighbors are looking after them. Karen is scared to hold them, but she tries her best.

Although I've known from the beginning that we're in good hands, I now write:

Don't know anything about the children.

And:

Marian unconscious.

Critical.

Don't keep alive artificially.

Then suddenly, in a muddle:

Certain people must be told.

Pink book in green box near tel. + 2 on my desk. Thanks.

The politeness is almost embarrassing: canceling my appointments so thoughtfully while you are dying. . . . But that's clinging to daily life, with which I have to go on — a survival instinct, isn't it? And to be honest, the admiration this evokes in many a visitor, however unjustly, is encouraging.

Poor Jack drives to our house and back again to get the documents I asked for — *he* can't tell how important they are. And Trish informs more friends, answers questions on the phone, goes and finds the right clothes for Rosemyn, cycles to school, takes care of their own three children, and makes coffee for a friend who's upset after her visit to you. She wonders aloud, "Aren't we in the way of the two families?"

But at our bedsides or in doorways and corridors, gratitude is expressed and friendships are forged.

Tuesday, December 15th

These days are just fragments of physical struggle and emotional worries about you and the children. I may rouse from unconsciousness for only a matter of minutes, but they're sharp as knives.

During one night, I heard Phoebe screaming.

Jack spends some time with Rosemyn again even before going to work. Is it out of modesty that he doesn't tell me about this?

Still writing on paper, I ask a nurse: *Can anyone visit Phoebe?*

And: *Does she know what's happening?*

Too hot.

When respirator off?

Breathing is harder; don't need to do that myself?

No, that's the crazy thing: I've got to concentrate on *not* breathing. Which makes me gasp with fear.

Believe what they say, Arno! Trust the machine!

Hollow under my back.

I've heard of bedsores, but so soon?

Can't pee well.

But again, I needn't. There's a catheter.

Is there a bell for emergencies?

It's on the rail above my head.

When the doctors remove blood and mucus from my lungs with an aspirator, the bell is no help. Apparently, the aspirator is inserted alongside the breathing tube — of which I wasn't aware before. I interrupt their work and motion for a sheet of paper again.

Is now in gullet.

Was fine but now I'm choking!

It's really too deep. I'm choking!

It causes a tickling cough, at least so it seems, which terrifies me. The sense of choking is so real that I squeeze their arms. I have to explain that my throat is blocked. But they don't understand. If only I could speak a few words! I can't pull myself free.

If only they had told me it just *feels* like choking! They know exactly what they're doing, so I need to be calm and surrender.

Come on, Arno, think of Marian!

Soon sedative. I'm worn out.

And soon it occurs to me that you must have felt even more helpless when you started breathing again, with courage born of despair and without knowing what was awaiting you, unable to squeeze arms or ask for pen and paper.

To think of you and be close to you is all I want, but my body's in the way.

Bit nauseous. Fatigue?

The tube not out? Try first?

Ever so politely I'm trying to tell the doctors what to do, trying to rouse pity and understanding — the way a dog licks the person who's coming to get it for more cruel experiments.

Scared of tickling cough.

Dog with Phoebe?

No dog?

Right. Nobody can be that stupid! But I did hear a dog. There's a whole sheet for two words: *So tired.*

So hot.

I bet the heat is turned up absurdly high.

Marian.

This must be a question, but I don't know to whom or what answer is given.

Does Ph. recognize you?

Phoebe.

There's always someone with you, Rose, and Phe, and somehow I can join them inwardly, so I should give up wanting things and surrender to the void consisting of love.

However, Mam and Dad have trouble reading the phrases I've written in crisscross lines. And anyway, it's ridiculous, what I'm asking them. Wilma is trying to contact us about a vacation address. But Mam and Dad have never heard of Wilma, and where has Jack put my notebook? I point to what I think is the bedside closet, but there is no closet, and my frustration hurts them to tears.

Never mind. Wilma can wait.

Phoebe is unconscious but needs support.

She can feel caress or closeness.

I've heard her plaintive cries: "No, no, no!"

I'm told she's pulled the feeding tube out a few times, and now, hearing her shrieks, I know the tube is being pushed back into her tiny nose.

Next time anesthetic please?

They explain it's not as bad as it sounds.

Her hands are tied down. She pulls them free again, even if she hasn't come around yet.

At least I've *asked* for the anesthetic, although it's dawning on me that I'm asking crazy questions. If I'm really brave and stay close to her inwardly, my presence might mean something to her.

The next minute, it seems as if heaven opens. From very far and yet very near, sounds come floating softly yet clearly from all directions, bringing peace and relief like the touch of fingertips does.

Ah, I remember: somebody was going to play the lyre for Phoebe, who has begun her long journey of awakening.

So Phe is at the heart of this calm.

Playing her lyre, Joan (who is a friend of a friend I don't even know) has difficulty separating her own emotions from what's going on with Phoebe. But it's drawing from emotions that gives music its value.

I need to let you know how hard people are working for us.

Somebody says your handbag is missing. Didn't you have it with you? Are the bankcards in it?

Your account is blocked.

But surely one doesn't steal from a nearly dead person in a car wreck?

Who has her things? I ask — without knowing myself what things I mean.

Several people are busy with the upper part of my body. Held forward, half-awake, I can hear them: "We're taking an X-ray of your chest."

Is this a memory of the night I was admitted?

It seems they've brought their equipment to my bed,

but perhaps I've been moved, tubes and all, to the X-ray department.

It's a lot of trouble, and I really can't cooperate.

I don't feel any pain until somebody leans more or less on my broken leg. And this person can feel something too, because her voice says, "Actually, what else has he got?"

Once more I'm held by a number of people who sigh and moan; they're having trouble. "Can't find it," the doctor says. "Sorry. That happens . . ."

He's talking about a spinal painkiller; there seems to be a difficult little spot for administering that.

They decide to roll me onto my side — on six broken ribs — and there's a pain that makes me think: So this is called "unbearable."

Don't! Stop!

Yet all I can do is groan as loudly as possible. They *know* it hurts. The doctor is uneasy, and he fails again.

It will be about six weeks before I can lie on my side in a reasonably comfortable way. Good thing I can lose consciousness from the pain.

Until they're back.

When they decide to put me into a sitting position this time, we're all terrified, and the doctor keeps saying, "Just one more sec. Sorry, so sorry, a very short moment . . ."

But, oddly enough, I don't feel too much now, and I'd like to reassure this kind man.

Those who drop by this afternoon get to read this:

Had a rough day. Now need cheering up.

I'd better make sure I'm part of day-to-day life. To live is what I want, apparently, or rather: life wants me, even though I don't do much for it; I'm just pulled along.

Marian in danger? I ask Lauren and Ernest.

By now they have prepared themselves. Their answers are sincerely careful, but I press on:

Living = probably serious damage. Doesn't register with me. I don't feel anything.

Worst: for the children, later.

Nurses are moved by you. So good. I do feel that!

Fortunately, everybody is allowed to decide for themselves how long they can stay with me; friends and family come and go. I sleep so deeply in between that I can handle a great deal, I think, and I promise to be honest and say when it's too much.

Phoebe — bad concussion.

Lauren explains that a brain contusion is more serious. Of course she does not explain that lasting damage should be expected.

Rose: What exactly has she got?

Then quickly back to Phoebe, because Rosemyn's arm will heal.

Important: As soon as she wakes, tell her I'm here but can't walk yet.

I can hear Phoebe, and I've all the time in the world to think.

You know: as Ph. is unconscious, they might forget her.

See, darling, don't worry: I'll take good care of them, with the help of others.

I don't know with whom, but confer: *Marian must not be a guinea pig. No endless operations.*

As if relatives had a say in this.

As if I'd *want* you dead.

I'm so glad I really know what I want and feel, for you as well as me. In many respects we used to be *one*, didn't we?

Go when you're ready, my love. You've fulfilled your task here, and your trust will not be betrayed.

How do her parents react?

They're tough, perhaps too much so. But yes, that may apply to me too. "Tough" is an unpleasant word.

Your mother's heart is not good at all. Still, she visits you every day.

Because she lost her own mother so early, in a time when there wasn't much room for coping with death (not a word said, all her things got rid of), this deepens her grief when she visits our children today. It shows when she comes to me and even tries to take away my feelings of guilt.

Annicka is one of your many friends who always seem to be on their way to the hospitals, going by bike to ours or by train to yours, or getting a lift from others.

Been to Rose now? Had a good time?

Due to Rosemyn's spontaneity and eccentricity, there's

often something funny going on, but she can also be straightforward about the accident. After all, she hasn't seen the three of us since then.

Sometimes her room is crowded. People want to come and see with their own eyes what they can't believe. You know Rose is a perfect hostess. She receives the numerous presents, talking expressively about her adventures. In a certain way she truly enjoys the attention and the distraction.

So that the moments of loneliness, before she goes to sleep, stand no chance of becoming real.

And so many people from the past have re-emerged that her notion of present and future must be confused.

R. here tomorrow.

Which I'm afraid to think of, since I can't speak.

I'll soon be off the machine.

I write it down, but a few months later, I won't remember this great new phase at all. Am I proud? Happy? Frightened?

One stage of recovery will quickly be followed by the next and vanish behind what's happening now.

List of visitors.

For the girls, I mean. A schedule is needed to create some calm and rhythm.

After seeing Phoebe, people often cry.

The "evening shift" read to them from carefully chosen picture books. They rub Rosemyn's cold feet and answer her probing questions, and they whisper to Phoebe in her sleep.

Rose interrogates Trudy about her daughter's death

and her ways of dealing with it. "What do you do on Hanny's birthday?"

Several women and older girls are given a mother's role: Rosemyn strokes and hugs them intimately. For Trudy these moments are good but hard. Her own process of mourning intensifies or starts all over again — and it was just recently that she found new ways to cope in life.

You have no idea what you've brought about in people, in wide circles, how their perceptions have changed. They give up their holidays and appeal to others in turn, partly because they see it as an honor rather than a sacrifice.

Jack and Trish keep coming at *all* hours, taking or bringing a bag of laundry. They've been in every corner of our house now — also under our pillows and under the leaking water heater.

Annicka has to wait outside when my breathing tube is removed. I can whisper! My lungs and I are doing our best, longing to be normal again.

Thinking back to this day, Annicka says, "Then, would you believe, you asked how I was doing. You knew exactly what was important to me."

Speaking for you.

Wednesday, December 16th

Phoebe sleeps restlessly, screaming, rubbing her head, and she can't be "corrected," as the nurses call it, with medication alone. Her head turns compulsively to the left. When she's awake for short spells, she says "No" and "Mammy." Her bed is put next to mine for a few minutes that escape me completely.

The days are a mist with mountaintops of consciousness breaking through.

Today's top is Rosemyn, who is brought from the other side of the hospital, in bed and traction and all, wheeled over by two nurses.

I'm totally powerless myself; that's the first thing I realize when I see and especially *feel* her eyes. They're groping for me, pleased, curious, shocked, knowing, concealing. They're watching my body — with IV drip and oxygen tube — and my soul, which is quite exposed as well, I guess.

The depth in her eyes must touch something in me that is deeper than memory: in a kind of mental reflex, out of very thin air, I say, "I'll never make jokes in the car again."

The nurses withdraw.

And this flash of lucidity withdraws for good into

oblivion. Nurse Janet will mention it to Lauren, who will not tell me about it until she's read this manuscript a year later. A lot of gaps were filled in by witnesses.

There's no witness right now, so I can't trace back everything we say — only what I recall myself.

"What've you got on your forehead?" Rosemyn asks.

"A wound. Scary?"

"All the blood . . . Does it hurt?"

"Nah. . . . How are you?"

"OK. Miss Erica came, and Miss May, and Karen and Rianne. . . . Will Mam get better?"

"I don't know."

"What do you think?"

"I really don't know."

"But what do you *think?*"

"Sweetheart, Mam's body is badly injured. I'm not sure if she *can* get well again."

"What's she got?"

"The worst kind of concussion. And inside her belly, a lot is broken."

Rosemyn's bed is alongside mine. Lying on my back, I turn my head as far as possible, but I can only see her askance and blurred, which hurts on two levels. Lying on her side, she can observe me pretty well. I think she asks everybody the same questions about you, so my responsibility increases. She goes on talking about visitors and presents and all the things she's seen on television.

After five minutes I'm exhausted, but I persevere for a while. Is TV the right thing now? The news? She was so used to our dosage. . . .

Your parents are with you in the morning, Judy at night and often in the afternoon. With her experience as a nurse, she can look after you and prepare you for the night; still, she'd like to be of more help.

Your condition is so serious that the short visiting hours in the afternoon must be strictly observed. This time is mainly for your friends. Sometimes they have to wait their turn, and only a couple of minutes are left for each, though unbounded love must be of vital importance.

When you move your head or a hand, they go through harrowing hope, especially during moments of meditation: Is it a new beginning of life or just a reflex that has nothing to do with your true self?

A nurse repeats that brain activity is nil.

Thea fights her wish to stay with you permanently. In her diary she writes, "You keep crying for help. You're very distressed and also say, 'Don't let me down.'" But she wonders to what extent this is actually a projection of her own emotion:

Dear Marian, your soul was far away. You weren't there at all. But we played some music for you, and your body did react a little. Where were you, my love?

When Annicka is there, she can feel your warmth, as if you're giving her a hearty welcome — encounters across physical borders. After this comes the shock of physical reality, leaving her adrift.

Not hiding her grief, she talks with you heart-to-heart about Rosemyn and Phoebe. But she also wonders if that's tormenting you, detaining you.

Holding your hand, she feels a slight reaction. Or is this what she *wants* to feel? Again, that question.

What's best for you? If we "let you go," you could feel abandoned; if we encourage you to stay, you might feel pressured.

In the corridor, Annicka runs into Lauren and says, "She'll come back."

"If only she can," Lauren says. "She's clinically dead."

Is it a clash between wish and reality or between hope and despair?

Annicka can't remember how she gets to the hospital cafeteria. Trudy is visiting too and takes her along. Everybody takes care of everybody these days.

When I wake up at the end of this morning, I'm conscious of my surroundings for the first time, probably because I've been moved. It's a big room with partitions formed by yellow curtains. Nice, that sunny yellow.

Seeing a number of very old, very ill people in the room, I try to stay sensible: I can simply look away, or the curtains around my bed can be drawn.

They must have told me something about this move, but I don't remember what. There's no one here now. I can't tell what ward or which floor this is. And while that's quietly sinking in, I start crying. I don't mind, I'm not ashamed, but it's awkward to signal to the arriving nurse and ask for a tissue. He gives me one of those fancy boxes we never buy. Details like this are continually diverting my attention from you.

I'm still waiting calmly for what is to come — without

realizing I've left Phoebe behind in the ICU — and then Feli is here, with kiwis. It's not even visiting hours! Kiwis are bursting with vitamins, aren't they?

I've met Feli only once. What a surprise; she came cycling all this way across town to see me. She dreaded this moment, and I'm enjoying her candid relief. Why should anyone dread seeing *me*?

She leaves to see Rosemyn next. It's wonderful how people go from one to the other of the three of us in this hospital, bringing the latest news and meeting friends along the way.

A plate is put in front of me: stew, with a colorful dessert.

Food?

I do feel a bit hungry and I'm happy about this new development, but a few bites will do. The woman who takes away the plate is very understanding.

I doze off again and come around in another ward. On my left, in this room for two, a man is talking on the phone in bed. After falling off his horse, he was kicked in the leg, but he's the manager of a huge business, and his work continues non-stop. This setting is more difficult for me than the room with the half-a-dozen dazed fellow patients.

My back hurts so badly that they decide to take another X-ray — to be on the safe side. A transport man unplugs my bed and pushes me through the corridors at a rapid speed. To me the air seems to be whooshing past, and it feels as if my lungs will shut down again. He parks me in a deserted hall on a different floor.

"They'll come for you in a minute."

I'm so tired that I'm really worried. I have breathing problems, feel the emptiness around me, but can't call for help. It must be a mental thing. *Stay calm, save oxygen.*

While the X-ray assistant does his job, I don't have the breath to tell him something's wrong.

He wheels me back into the hall and says, "They'll come for you in a minute."

It's more like ten or twenty.

I feel like I'm being suffocated, but why now? Nerves? Loneliness? Is my psyche shaken?

These transport men are terribly busy, moving from one task to the next as assigned, covering about fifteen miles a day in the hallways and corridors. They aren't medical personnel. After the journey back, both my bed *and* the oxygen tube are plugged in neatly again.

I didn't even know there was a tube in my nose.

I'm given a single room, 512, although this extravagance is not supposed to be covered by the insurance we've paid for.

I feel a strange kind of nostalgia for what I've left behind, for the care I received both awake and asleep in the ICU, which seems an era in itself.

Naturally, the sympathy and privileges have to do with our situation — the children should be able to come and see me at all hours — but the offered facilities are not matter of course.

Rosemyn would like to come again tonight, but I'm too tired.

All I've got left from the ICU is the foam-rubber slippers that protect my heels against bedsores. I'm still permanently on my back, which is rubbed with a special oil.

How is that going with you, my darling? They can't oil your back, can they? How your body must be in your way; I guess you really have had enough of it.

In the course of the days you get horrible bruises, still caused by inner injuries. My own discomfort seems insignificant by comparison, and I feel ashamed of all the attention it's given. I don't exactly know what they do to you, or what machines you're on, but that's not the point now. You're fighting in a different dimension, I hope. If only I could do something for you, anything more useful than staying myself, having faith, and saving my strength for the children.

Spontaneously, a "circle of light" has been formed for you that links people of all beliefs and experiences. Your friends invite their friends to be still and turn their attention to you at half past seven each evening.

Never mind what it's called: meditation, prayer, concentration, being with you in thoughts. . . . It happens with the purest intensity. But of course, you know what I mean — you've felt it.

Thursday, December 17th

Phoebe is ready for the pediatric ward. She'll be sharing a big, light room with Rosemyn. She goes on sleeping — fortunately — and from a dozen feet away, hanging in traction but moving like a hooked fish, Rosemyn keeps watch over her with such devotion that she often annoys the staff. She has a rough time when Phoebe is crying or screaming.

The two of them are a team here. Phe is sheer fragility, largely in the spiritual world, close to you, from whom she can't break away. Rose is down to earth, alert, all senses acute, all memories intact. Her directness may get Phe back: she's always there to welcome her with a loud voice and dark, fiery eyes.

"Phoebe?"

No answer.

"Phoebe! Do you want me to read to you?"

Groan.

"One day . . ."

"Phe? Do you want me to sing to you?"

No answer.

Then comes a summer or a winter song, a Christmas or an Easter hymn.

In that room, the attention of visitors is rudely divided. Rosemyn claims them from the doorway, drawing them past Phoebe, who needs the subtlest balance between closeness and distance. They hardly dare come near Phe, let alone touch her, and they whisper their way toward her.

When Karen asks Phe if she recognizes her, she suddenly says, "Laura and Mary." Then, "You are sweet." And "Christmas tree."

This could be a sign that her memory's returning, because last weekend she and Rosemyn admired that early tree at Karen's with envy and surprise.

Such great, unexpected news is phoned around — and we're all afraid to believe it.

After my first breakfast, I'm worried about their meals. The fresh slices of bread become a ball of fat in my mouth. I can deal with that, but what's my body supposed to do with it?

I'm also worried about the amounts of candy they get (boxes and baskets of it) from loving visitors eager to comfort them.

I know there are bigger problems, but the responsibility for this has fallen on me. Food has to do with health. And if I think about what they used to get from you . . .

The physical therapist, Peter, teaches me how to breathe deeply again, which is crucial for the future of my lungs. His admiration of my achievements is so real that I'm prouder than I have been in a long time. But the credit is completely yours, since you once asked me, as casually as possible, to read a fragment in your yoga book. You didn't show me much of what you loved to do in the alternative health field (you knew better), but one or two occasions affected the rest of my life.

When there's a deep, soft hawk in my throat, Peter's face clouds over. I'll have to cough up the remainder of mucus in my lungs.

No! I just won't breathe deeply again!

But Peter tells me the mucus would cause something like pneumonia. That could develop next week, given my recent drafty trip through the corridors. . . .

After inhaling once more, in spite of myself, I feel a cough coming. I *have* to cough, because down in the bronchi something is in the way, but I *can't* — not with broken ribs! Just like one can't play football on a broken leg, can one?

I venture a mild kind of cough. That already makes me feel like I'm torn to pieces, but it's not effective. This lump will have to be hauled up violently, and no doctor can help. In fact, the coughing impulses come naturally, so quitting or putting it off is useless. It does help that I can feel by the centimeter what progress I'm making.

This takes half the morning. Finally a ball of phlegm and blood comes out, which I catch in my hand. The following hours are blissful. Now I can handle anything! Surely I'm cured and I'll never be ill again! Until — oh, haughtiness! — I take an extra-deep breath and recognize the hawk from far down.

This time it helps that Lauren is here. If I am to perform these acts of valor, there may as well be a spectator. She catches the next ball in a plastic cup.

Each time is the last time — I'm sure of it! But the whole business takes a day or two. What a good thing I didn't know that beforehand.

The catheter is removed, since "the bladder of a young chap shouldn't get lazy," according to a lady surgeon doing the rounds. OK, sure — the fewer tubes, the better. I'm frightened all right, peeing in this position, because I can't press, even though the strain is increasing. But never mind. As soon as my bladder is full enough, it will run easily, I guess.

For the time being, I'll be distracted by other pains, by visits from Rosemyn, the mail, other visitors. . . .

Twice a day, Rose comes to my room for about twenty minutes. Speaking and seeing cost a great deal, and undergoing her gaze costs a lot more. She asks, pleads, begs, piercing a silence that's more fearful than her voice. She expects everything from me. What else does one have a mam and dad for? But she crushes my whispering impotence. Phoebe lies nearly lifeless beside her, and you are even more sick — that's what we told her — so she can draw her own conclusions.

To her, these visits are always too short, since what she's coming for — something to hold on to — is not given. We do hold hands for a while, but in such a clumsy way. . . .

The bell I ring is merciless.

"Bye, Dad. When can I come again?"

"Oh, sweet, I don't know. As soon as possible, all right?"

"OK. Tonight?"

"I hope so."

"Good. See you tonight."

At this moment, Raymond is the one who gives me the support I'll soon have to pass along. Every minute of his time is spoken for, booked, but he's come here, all the way from Hammerford, at the very hour of an appointment we made weeks ago. He's going to see you as well, which does me tremendous good.

His presence is sufficient in and of itself. I don't remember his exact words. His quietness, kindness, and acceptance, which are sublime *within* the ordinary and vulnerable, have lasting effects. He "opens" me to a fundamental inspiration (taboo to our intellect) by which I was first touched — blind and deaf — through you.

The way he tells me I have enough strength, or something to that effect, makes me *accept* it, literally take it in. After this, I feel embarrassed by other people's surprise at "my" courage.

When Thea is with you this afternoon, she observes a coughing and swallowing movement, and you seem to be shaking your head.

"How sad you were," she writes in her diary. "I talked to you, told you I was there. Marian, how great you are — a comfort to many."

Nurse Geoff says I may go to you by ambulance, and he warns me about the well-known regret to come if I don't. But just the thought of the trip and my uselessness has drained all my energy. Besides, despite the ten miles between us, I can feel your greatness, and you probably know exactly what's going on in me. In any case, there's no regret now, only hunger for the warmth and comfort of the physical. It would be good to *say* what we already know.

How I'd like to re-live certain times, to say more and be silent differently. There was a lot available that I didn't give you.

So here's where the regret is, from before.

A number of friends meet in the waiting area outside your room. They don't want to claim your attention. They let Judy go in first and give her all the time she needs.

It's impressive and significant, how people *long* to be with you, even including your damaged body.

At the girls' school, there are more instances of serious illness and death. After long hesitation the board decides not to cancel the Christmas service — or celebration.

Phoebe would have been an angel.

Her costume is ready on a coat peg at home.

Friday, December 18th

The nights are difficult. I have trouble sleeping on my back, but I can't position myself any other way. My head keeps falling sideways; I want to nestle, fold, or turn over, but my whole body is in the way.

Although it's a kind of defeat, I take a sleeping pill for the first time in my life; otherwise getting through the day would be impossible. But now I'm tossing about, or the bed is fooling around with me. I'm heavy yet floating while my body stays where it is. Nausea or headache is pleasant compared to this alien torture. But there's nothing to be done; there's no antidote except submission — waiting until it's worn off.

As soon as I'm awake enough to act, I press the bell above my bed. Finally, here's someone I can talk to!

The relief makes me cry.

It must be some sort of allergic reaction, but that can only be discovered by trial and error. The nurses don't comment (do they think I'm hysterical?), but Annicka tells me she sleeps tight with a Seresta, and for tonight a Seresta is ordered.

Phoebe is so wild that they take her to another room.

Rosemyn wakes up from the pain in her arm, and she's given half a Paracetamol.

At six, Phe's awake and clearheaded. After an explanation, she accepts the frightful thing called "feeding tube" — pushed in just like that? — and may return to the room she shares with Rose. But she hates being washed.

The neurologist drops by. Phoebe can have a pillow, and when a nurse is present, her hands can be untied. She ought to drink something before each drip feed.

She sleeps a lot but groans and screams now and then.

During a rare lucid spell, somebody reads to her, and she likes that. To some questions she gives good answers, but other "remarks" make no sense at all.

I'm so glad it's daytime! The days are exhaustingly full of diversion. My temperature is taken, breakfast arrives, I'm bathed. There are exercises and doctor's visits. Flowers, a fruitbasket, and a pile of mail are brought in.

Wilma writes, "I called several times and didn't understand why there was no answer in the evenings."

The phone in that poor empty house of ours: it might ring a hundred times, hoping to find life. Can the neighbors hear it? A gruesome idea. Good thing I've tried so hard to reach people. Has everybody been informed now?

No. Henry, Nell and Emily, Eric the rambler . . . He likes making surprise visits. I can just see him with his bike on the doorstep, waiting, wondering, choosing a new destination and trying again later, till the neighbors talk to him or till we're mentioned somewhere by mutual friends.

In the mail from home are two Christmas cards and

extremely sunny greetings from the Canary Islands. These don't disturb me at all. We are just a minute aspect of life. Christmas and the Canaries can hardly stop existing because we had an accident, because you are now in that space between life and death, an empty phase of indecision. Who can wake you up and show you the way?

While heaven is meeting you, I think the world should stop turning and pause with awe to support you. But so many sacrifices are made, large and small ones, that the world has no time to acknowledge them: too many people are dying slowly. You see, Mar, I do have lapses of gloom. Will soon be over, OK? At least you can count on absolute frankness.

One of the gifts I receive is a children's book for all ages, *The Whale's Song,* which I unwrap with Rosemyn. I have no time for reading, no strength to read out loud. And yet, a picture book with a story for which few words suffice, about trust going beyond coincidence . . .

With great ease and speed, life can move from supreme themes to the most primary needs. I still can't pee, and the pressure is too great now, both in my mind and in my belly. There is some sympathy for this problem, but the only solution is to reinsert the catheter. This isn't easy either, because of the pressure that's built up.

Obviously, I'm scared and embarrassed. It takes three nurses and a phone call to the doctor. "Usually I'm quite good at it," says one of those who fail.

They don't succeed until I've had a dose of Doryl. My penis will be black for weeks. And visitors always see the bag of urine beside my bed. Compared to this experience, the changing of a drip needle, to prevent infection, is a trifle, just like the notorious injections against thrombosis. And then once more, ashamed, I think of you: a decision is being made about life and death.

Today Rosemyn has to do without her dad. After conquering fear and pain, I have nothing left for her. Even harsher is the knowledge that it doesn't occur to Phoebe to ask for me — *if* she were able to ask for anything.

They offer her some custard and applesauce. She tries the applesauce but doesn't like it. Her teeth can't be brushed either; she keeps her mouth shut tight.

The team of specialists around you have decided you'll stay on the life-support system. We're all baffled: What are you doing? What do you want yourself? Why is it taking so long? Are the machines keeping you here against your will?

My love, do you want me to take action? But I don't know whether I'll have a say in this, or where I could begin. Besides, perhaps you're still fighting for life on earth — for a specific, wonderful reason. . . . *My* longing to be together again is sometimes overwhelming.

Our bond seems based on a love of timeless times.

To which we'll return, of course.

See you then, see you soon and always, in whatever form.

When I'm trying to console Rosemyn with the image that you're among angels, passing on strength to us, she shouts, "Mam shouldn't do that! She has to keep it all to herself, because she needs it more!"

Thea would like to see you tonight, but at six o'clock she's told on the phone that your condition is critical. You're having trouble taking in the oxygen. This morning, she noticed you gave counter-pressure. Your parents are with you now.

If you don't even take oxygen from the machine, it's clear what you want — which confirms my first feeling.

You need stronger respiration than women normally get; you're swallowing and foaming at the mouth, as if refusing the tube.

Thea calls your father at nine p.m. and learns you need rest. In her eyes, that really means you need to have complete rest, to leave your physical existence. There's a visiting ban, because tomorrow your parents will stay with you all day.

Worried, Thea asks how she can keep in touch.

"Call again next week," says your father.

She doesn't know what to do. After she confers with other friends, the decision is made to do nothing except concentrate on "the light" around you, your parents, and the doctors.

It's their expression: to *hold you in the light* or *carry you to the light*. And after I get used to it, I think it's beautiful.

Saturday, December 19th

At about three in the morning, I wake up from the pain in my back. Intuitively, I know nothing's wrong: the X-rays were all right, and in the daytime I'm fine. But the pain is unbearable, and I think that nothing can be done about it. Again, it's crazy that I've completely forgotten there's a bell I can ring, even in the dead of night, when only the devil himself seems to be still active.

So this is desperation: being lost in fear and failing to ask for help.

I don't know what makes me remember the bell in the end.

After some hesitation, the nurse goes and checks to see if I can have a suppository. I tell her honestly that I've never had one before and don't know how to do it. So she does it for me.

What a miracle drug: after twenty minutes I don't feel anything and fall asleep.

Until it's worn off. But now I can hear sounds in the corridor, morning sounds of fellow human beings, and with my watch at hand, I'll manage till breakfast.

Toast, yogurt, and tea make me the Prince of Daybreak, feasting on fearlessness, and cheerfully I greet everyone entering my realm.

The spinal anesthetic appears to have "perished," and they won't insert a new one. I'm allowed to take a fair amount of Paracetamols, but I don't need any. Nurse Geoff insists, doesn't understand when I refuse, thinks I want to be the tough guy, but during the day I don't feel much pain. Probably the Seresta makes me fall into an unnaturally deep sleep, maybe lying in a bad position, so when a muscle is stressed, the pain builds for hours before waking me up.

I can't cope any longer with the searching look in Rosemyn's eyes. There's so much fear and loneliness, in contrast with her loud, anecdotic talking, that I'd be letting her down if I didn't share my feelings about your having to leave. It's an aggravating weakness: I dread hurting her, but it doesn't work any longer to reason that medically everything is still possible and that a preparation for death would be unfair to both you and her.

For days she has avoided the question: Why isn't Mam brought here?

She's asked Leon, "Do *you* know what Mam's got?"

How characteristic of her to choose him; he stands for frankness.

But the medical facts are of no use to her.

She's afraid to look me in the eye, she withdraws into darkness, and I know what needs to be done. And now that I'm absolutely sure, I'm not scared anymore, at least not in that paralyzing way.

"Hey," she says, "a phone!"

"Yes. Great, isn't it?"

Have you called Denton yet? she's asking inwardly, yet visibly.

I can't think of any introduction or roundabout way to do what I must, so I just say, "I have to tell you that Mam can't get better. She's going to die. She's going back to heaven, to the light."

Rosemyn cries angrily, "No! I don't *want* her to! She's not going to die — you can never be sure! Why did you cause the accident?"

"I didn't. I mean, not on purpose. An accident *happens.*"

"But Mam doesn't want to die, either. Because we wouldn't have a mother!"

"Yes, for your sake, Mam wants to stay, I'm sure. Maybe that's why it's taking so long. But her body's all broken."

"What's wrong, then?"

I explain. "Her brain is almost dead already. If she were to live, she might not be able to walk or speak. . . . She has to continue on her way, and that's now leading to heaven. Which is really a good thing for her."

"But not for us."

"No. For us it's difficult. And Mam *knows* that. It's terrible for her as well."

"So you can't know for sure that she's going to die. . . ."

"No, but I *think* so. We must wait and get strong. And inside, you can always talk with Mam."

I'm forced to use words. I can't give her a hug or take her on my lap and rock her, to console both of us. I can only pass her the tissues from my box, and I need to concentrate on that so hard that day-to-day worries claim all my attention again.

Alex and Phyllis take her back to 6 East. There she can hug them and cry and talk for as long as she wants. "I've always known it, or else Mam wouldn't have stayed in Denton. It's nice that she's going to the light, because she won't hurt anymore, but I'm also kind of jealous."

It's another weekend; uncles and aunts have traveled far for us again. They shuttle back and forth between the wards, get me coffee with hot milk, eat my sweets, and carefully show joy or concern about the children, whom they listen to or read to and caress — like a mother or father.

Jack will bring me new underwear. What size did I take? Make it extra large; that's more comfortable in bed. (How much longer will I have to stay in bed?) And white is always practical. . . . He buys the old-fashioned kind, big and durable, which I'm ashamed of at first and glad of later: they're nicely warm and solid. Is he aware that *you* used to buy those for me?

Phoebe can eat some porridge, but she refuses. She does drink a bit of water. Her teeth are brushed with difficulty.

I'm finding out about Phe's existence in summary sentences from others, and the messengers often got the information from one of the nurses. "Her drip feed is now 200. . . ." Is that a good thing? I'm also pleased to hear that she's got this feeding tube, because it means she needn't be forced to eat.

Phe's ordeals are something I can't bear to know about yet. And she's not imposing herself.

Sometimes Rosemyn carries a big shield, but she can also show her feelings.

In a nurse's report:

She knows her mother will soon die, and she's often overcome by sadness. Preoccupied with death. Jealous of Mam, who has a lot of light around her now. Dreads being alone. Her sister was put beside her, which she enjoyed. She feels responsible for Phoebe. Drinking went well, eating less. This I let be, because of her grief. Rosemyn didn't eat lunch, either.

The children's nurses propose that Rose and I go to say good-bye to you together. Rose doesn't know about it.

This afternoon your father calls Thea himself to let her know your friends can visit you again, which is much better news for us all than he presumably knows.

But WHAT is detaining these doctors?

They say that medically and mentally a recovery is still possible, but I don't think it is meant to be.

Nurse Bea takes a seat on the windowsill at my bedside. From the beginning I've been struck by her pureness and directness, revealing a quiet, inner depth. She's fully herself, even now as she's come to deal with a delicate personal matter. She looks at me calmly and says, "Have you talked to Rosemyn?"

I forgot she knew about that.

"Yes. . . ."

"Wouldn't it be good to see her again today?"

I must have stared — astonished and ashamed: Why didn't I think of this myself?

She leaves like a messenger, ready for a long journey back.

Rosemyn is brought at six o'clock, and how valuable Bea's suggestion was! She clutches at me with her eyes and her words. Of course — how would she sleep in that hospital room after just one discussion about her mother's death? She wants to say, ask, and hear everything again, testing whether I'll be wholly present, strong and attentive enough, not for two parents, but for one who's really there, with whom she can share.

As long as we're talking, we're tough.

Which shouldn't be.

Which doesn't work for long.

Phoebe looks up when people come into the room, and she nods when they say good-bye. But she refuses to eat. According to Rosemyn, she says she doesn't need to eat because food will come through the tube. According to the nurse, Rose is stimulating her not to eat.

Tonight, she vomits. *Told you*, Rose must be thinking. The nose/stomach tube comes out through her mouth! They decide not to insert a new one, to give her stomach a rest.

Her teeth are brushed under protest.

Exhausted, she falls asleep.

In a way this isn't helping you, of course. But again I

think you want to hear the whole truth about everything, since only that will help you ultimately. It means you can count on me for better or worse.

Nurse's report: *Just before bedtime, Rosemyn gets very emotional. She'd like to see her father.*

And bed and all, they wheel her over again.

"Cruel, isn't it," I say, "that you can't stay."

I'm stroking her hand.

How can two or three discussions about a mam's death be adequate?

Father is given the offer to stay the night with Rosemyn. Father declines.

I can't, my faraway daughter — I'm just too ill!

"That's very kind of your nurses, but I'll need to be alone and make phone calls and all kinds of arrangements. . . . I'll work hard to get better! All right? We'll have to persevere now, and it will cost us our utmost, but I'm sure we can do it."

Sucking her thumb, Rose thinks for a minute. "OK."

Rosemyn fell asleep quietly at 20.30. I've told her she can ring when she can't sleep and wants to talk. Rosemyn would like to have a photo of her mother.

Sunday, December 20th

Rosemyn wakes up in the middle of the night and talks about the crash. "It was the fault of those people who didn't paint the curbs white, and not Dad's."

Nurse's report: *On the one hand, she said her mother's soul is already with the angels and will come back to earth later, and they can live here in the meantime, the three of them (Rose, her father, and Phoebe). She'd like to go to her mother's funeral, if that's possible (but she thinks it isn't). On the other hand, she feels "inside" that her mother is going to get better.*

And to reassure both you and me:

Rosemyn was very happy with the visits to her father.

At six in the morning, Phoebe refuses the applesauce they're trying to feed her. Tea fails as well. The tube is put in again.

While her bed is being made, she lies in Rosemyn's bed for a bit, and that news reaches me quickly. I can just picture Rose trying to hug Phe, who'll curl up and nestle and sleep, not exactly meeting Rose's need for activity.

Lauren, Alex, and Phyllis go to look for photos in our house. It's one of those moments that are described only briefly in this account, but it's a most profound experience for these three.

The photo albums seem to be ready and waiting; you had been working on them for days before the accident. Three photos of you and the girls are in a small folder, perfectly ready to be taken along to the hospital. In the pictures, you are so close and cozy and unsuspecting, it's really tough for them to see. They also discover two photo frames lying on my desk: very recent presents to me from you.

They select some clothes for the girls, and in the bathroom Phyllis notices there's laundry in the washing machine. You must have switched it on before we got into the car.

She hangs it out in the loft hallway.

The photos are put into the frames, to be hung between the hospital beds of the children.

Staff and visitors talk about you out loud. The question is what Phoebe can hear and understand. More than may be observed, we think, and that hurts me. I'd want to tell her everything while she's on my lap, to show her with my hands and eyes and all my heart that we'll be all right. Then again, the way this is going now is quite natural, don't you think? Rosemyn stays close to Phoebe with everything she's got, including all her emotions and her loud voice. Phe must be dealing with this before she's fully awake.

At lunchtime there are French fries, and would you believe it: Phoebe eats a few too. That news both delights and worries me. Anyway, it sounds like an endearing sight — she must have thought: *What's this again?*

Nurse's report: *We think it's in protest that Phoebe doesn't eat or speak. She can but won't.*

Peter, the physical therapist, and nurse Geoff have put me in a chair at the table at the other end of my room. I don't remember for what purpose, but I feel heroic, and I want to stay here till Rosemyn comes.

She's brought by Alex and Phyllis, and they'll be able to ring the bell for me, says Geoff before leaving with Peter, in case of . . . Never mind. I've stopped listening.

But after a while, Alex and Phyllis retire respectfully, since Rose and I have such difficult things to discuss.

Although I strain myself a little, sitting upright at the table, we're enjoying this new phase immensely because now, for one thing, we can see each other properly. And the hardest part is over: facing and *saying* the worst.

When I badly need to get back in bed, I realize the bell is over the bed — at the other end of the room. Those who are always maneuvering the beds find my room rather small, but to me it seems huge right now.

Rose and I start laughing, partly from nerves, I suppose, and partly because our senses of humor are identical. We give a yell, of course — that is, Rose does — but the walls are thick, and the thick door is shut tight — perfect privacy! We can't hear a thing from outside, and no one comes in. Were lots of other bells rung just now, or is this break time for the staff?

From the lounge further down the corridor, Alex keeps checking the light above my door: it will be on if I press the bell. He's too discreet to knock on the door spontaneously.

I decide to show our daughter she's got a terrific dad: brave, strong, and resourceful. I stand up and start a kind of shuffling journey on one foot alongside the railing bars of her bed. No sooner is the sweat running down my back — at bar two — than my penis is stuck with a shock: the plastic bag attached to the catheter lies motionless and uncooperative behind a leg of the table at which I sat so proudly.

Oh, vanity!

I won't put up with this — not from a bag of urine. I move back and pull it along by the tube. It's a risky effort, demanding the last reserves of my energy, and I'm rigid with concentration.

After the railing of Rosemyn's bed — let's regard her silence as a token of awe — come several feet of empty space. No doubt I'm floating at heights of glory now, so that I make it to my bed with superhuman help, but for punishment or at least as a warning, those angels ought to shake my good knee.

I sink down on my bed and need some minutes to recover before I can reach for the bell. Then it proves to be silent: since the bed was moved, the plug is out.

Rose and I are flat on our backs with laughter, weakness, and anxiety.

Just when Rose prepares to call out again (usually her

voice is a cannon, isn't it?), Alex's concern overcomes his politeness.

Nurse's report: *Rosemyn's behavior is pretty changeable: first she talks about ordinary things; then two seconds later, she's very emotional. When alone, she often rings the bell.*

Phoebe looks at people but shows no other reactions and doesn't want to eat. She's very restless in her sleep.

Visitors report this, and I, along with them, am getting very worried about her, despite the French fries and the few moments of lucidity she's had. It's just as if she panicked when she came to: strange surroundings, a lot of familiar and unfamiliar people, no mam or dad. Especially no mam.

What would she do without you?

No, better to leave *with* you.

She withdraws, pines away — we're losing her. Both of you really deserve to be together, but it's unbearable to consider such a loss.

Monday, December 21st

Phoebe's relapse upsets everyone. She doesn't make any sort of contact, just lies there, moaning. When Annet, the recreational therapist, returns after the weekend, she advises the medical team to have Phoebe taken to me. And once more I wonder: Why for heaven's sake didn't I think of that myself? But OK, this will make me appreciate other people's sensitivity all the more. I didn't know better; all I knew was that Phoebe was scarcely in this world.

It's incredible that somebody can just wheel her to me in her bed, into and out of elevators and everything. . . . It must be a frightening trip for her, but if it helps her realize I'm still here. . . .

She arrives asleep, curled up like a little nothing, and she cries when she's lifted out of her nest. Tired, happy, awkward, and curious — like a new mother — I'm looking on.

Your Phoebe.

After eight days apart, I expect recognition and joy from her, but she's totally absent.

On my back, I'm stuck between drip and catheter; where is she supposed to lie? I'm trying to move up, but the tubes don't follow, every muscle screams, I'm losing my breath, start sweating. . . . She's already here, as small and soft as a baby. Not seeing me, she's trying to find a place, wriggling and bumping into me. I'd like to nestle with her, my arms embracing her. . . . Why won't she calm down?

She turns her back toward me, curls up, and sleeps with her head on the drip tube in my forearm.

As best I can I move her head to my upper arm, trying to pillow her there, which is a problem, since that area hasn't an ounce of fat. Then I'm finished. It's even hard to be happy. My Phoebe, who's known me for six years now, has turned away from me, has no idea where she is. But she seems to be peaceful, so I'd better relax myself and try to get a better sense of what she's feeling. Maybe she happens to be more comfortable on her left side. Or she simply turned toward the window, to light and space.

She protests when she's taken back, so I'm somewhat relieved.

Rosemyn is in the playroom, painting and playing with the magnet board. She talks to Annet about you, but at a certain point she thinks it's enough and goes into her shell.

From now on, Phoebe will be brought to me twice a day and Rosemyn only after dinner, which is not enough. The hours tend to be filled according to what's *not* possible.

After being washed, Phoebe dries her face herself. She won't eat, but she licks the jam off her fingers and sits on nurse Janet's lap for a while. She likes that, provided it doesn't happen too often.

I envy Janet because she's closer to Phoebe.

Tonight, however, they can't get through to her. She refuses food, turns her head away, and vomits after the drip feed.

Rosemyn says she's glad for you and other people who die. Because you're not in pain any longer.

Her arm hurts, and she gets half a Paracetamol.

A group from the Salvation Army has come to sing Christmas carols in the lounge, and I can go there by bed. I decline the offer but have my door left open so that the carols reach me from a safe distance. Even here it's difficult to find a way between aversion and emotion.

Once more, nurse Geoff urges me to go to Denton — possibly with Rosemyn. To encourage you? To say good-bye? He's even made a phone call and thinks I need to be prepared for your situation.

I will think about it, but my feelings already speak loudly: I'll do what I can for the *children* and make sure I get well, convinced that the minutes they spend in my presence are vital to both of them. And that you are watching eagerly, approving of my decision, in spite of your misery.

I've heard you're running a fever and are given antibiotics, which is horrible! Are you being violently stopped from leaving? Surely the fever — warmth! — is a better way of dying than unplugging the machines?

Please, let nature take its course.

You have to lie naked, to be dabbed with alcohol.

That hurts me like an irreverence.

I'm so worried and angry now that late in the evening I phone Raymond. I don't really know what I expect from him, but he always helps, and something has to be done.

He says I can ask you inwardly what's going on, what you're waiting for, what you expect from *me*. He happens to be at home and happens to have time (remarkably enough), and he'll guide me in meditation. We'll need to keep a close watch on our integrity: personal interests, such as our wish to keep you here, mustn't interfere. This requires a strict kind of concentration, even for Raymond.

It sounds strange and hard, something for experienced devotees. What makes him think I can do that? I've never done anything of the kind before. I've called him out of despair; I don't ask for help that easily.

He emphasizes that I'll have to do this myself, and slowly I realize he knows what he's doing.

Just as if he's giving directions to a driver, he tells me step by step what to do: concentrate fully on my breathing, empty myself of everything else, especially of thoughts, and be still at the top of each long breath. Then I can ask you my questions directly.

We hang up, and I ask a nurse to light a candle, explaining that it's for you. She goes to get permission (candles are not allowed) and brings a tea-light kind. Soon it's burning safely and beautifully in the glass tulip that was one of the first presents I got here.

I'm thinking: It won't work; I'll fail.

Still, I really try to submit to something beyond me. You talked about this sort of meditation. But (a technical question) how can I tell when I've reached full concentration?

Breathing deeply is what I normally do to conquer sleeplessness, and now I have to tell myself: Stay awake, eyes open! Seeing the room tends to disturb me, but looking and seeing don't matter, I believe, as long as I don't *think*.

Finally, when I do feel "empty" and open, I say out

loud, timidly, "Dear Marian, I love you. Everything is all right. Will you please show me you're here?"

With my eyes open, I can see you at the foot of the bed, not walking but slowly going here and there; two realities are merging! You have long, loose hair. You're about sixteen years old, shy yet coquettish, insecure yet superior. You don't speak, but what you're indicating is, "If you *want* me, I need to know what I'm worth to you. . . ."

I ask, "What do *you* want? How are you?"

The same girl is leaping, floating, dancing in meadows on the high coast of a country like Wales, where we had such a good time together, where you had this strong sense of origin. The fields are very high — I can only see grass and sky. Your hair is dancing along with you. It's you, but so new and independent that you're the very image of freedom. You do see me, but I'm nothing to you: less than air. That numbs me with fear, but it has nothing to do with arrogance, only the freedom — or "freedness" — that you deserve and that is so full of love. I understand enough before this reality fades back into the earthly one, where I can be both proud of myself and emotional.

I've done it; you came! You think I'm worth it, good enough for my task.

I love you so.

Tuesday, December 22nd

I ask for the phone number of Denton Hospital.

Your dedicated visitors have told me that they have to put on sterile coats before entering your room, and that the door opens with a special handle. The unit is noisier and less private than ours here. Due to renovations in progress, tools and materials are lying around in the corridors. But the nurses look after you with love and subtle care. I admire them, because even though they seem preoccupied with machines, they're really focused on you, of whom they know only your battered body.

You are very susceptible to atmosphere, can *create* an atmosphere better than anyone. Indeed, according to many, you still do: they feel a warmth in your room that must be spiritual. Undoubtedly, they're not only receivers, although that's how they experience it.

Doctor Lohmann, the neurologist, is making her rounds, busy all the time, but suddenly she's on the line: a soft, modest, agreeable voice. As the head of a team, she's responsible for you and a spokeswoman to your parents and Judy. They've told me about her striking, delicate appearance.

I have only one thing to say: "Please, don't leave her on the machines unnecessarily."

She explains: Your fever indicates infections, probably caused by the tubes.

But if even those instruments irritate your body . . .

She's listening carefully, and it's clear you're in good, humane hands. That reassures me to some extent, but again I tell her expressly that in this situation I'm not in favor of the life-support system. Then I ask, "You do think in terms of body and soul?"

"Yes."

"Could the connection become so thin that the soul could lose control over the body and would then be unable to leave it?"

"Yes."

"So that's the risk of this treatment: the notorious, endless comas?"

"Yes."

She doesn't hesitate or stop to think; she's heard me out and understands me perhaps emotionally rather than intellectually.

A lot of people focus their supportive thoughts on your doctors, wishing them wisdom, so that their decisions will correspond with your inner progress.

Every morning, Joan comes to play the lyre, now for Rosemyn and Phoebe together. She plays "A Flower Is Springing" by Praetorius, and "Von Himmelhoch" in the rocking, rhythmical way of the solo in Bach's Christmas Cantata. Rosemyn asks for the song about heaven opening in the middle of a winter's night, and that's exactly what it feels like from time to time: you bring about some sort of fusion of heaven and earth, which will have to be of lasting value: we'll have to sustain it.

As well as she can, Rosemyn washes herself, and she makes a deal with the nurses: she'll drink six glasses of lemonade every day.

Rosemyn was in a good mood. She was less meddlesome toward Phoebe and enjoyed herself in the playroom. Does talk a lot about her mother.

At other moments, she's loud, boisterous, and moody.

Phoebe's taken for an X-ray to see if she can have a bath soon. The wideness of her pupils is a consequence of her injuries, and the fact that she won't eat is still a symptom as well, says the neurologist. Thanks very much! Could have told the staff that sooner! Eating and drinking should not be forced on her; she's vomited again.

Because of that, her morning visit to me has to be skipped (which means an extra one for Rosemyn). Phe's shoulders and hips are red from lying in bed so much. (I'm glad I won't learn about that until months later.) In spite of everything, I'm told, her mind is clearer than it was yesterday, and she answers some questions. When a picture book is read to her, she's all attention, but she takes no interest in toys, not even in her own dolls.

I inform the nurses that Phoebe is a poor eater in general and that she's terribly shy. They insist I tell her about your condition as soon as possible. This bothers me, but I assume that the right words will come at the right time, as they did with Rosemyn.

In the afternoon, Phoebe seems to recognize me vaguely, but I mustn't impose my happiness on her. The very air is new to this six-year-old baby: she makes grabbing movements at it, looking disturbed. She also pulls at my wedding ring and at the railing of the bed.

I'm glad she's moving at all, though. I can't wait to give her a long, tight hug, but that would crush her.

By the time she's nestled and fallen asleep, I'm tired too, just singing or humming something — only her name, really, in the lowest voice.

As she's sleeping, she suddenly says, "It's good."

Hearing her voice for the first time, I can hardly believe she said it herself. In her sleep! It feels as if you were looking on and gave your opinion, but does it make a difference?

With the courage I receive from this, I tell her you won't get better and will be "staying with the angels," but we will do well.

I can't find the courage to use the word *die,* which is like a defeat to me. Actually, it's only Rosemyn's knowing and talking that have pushed me as far as this. Is it a great mercy that Phoebe hears it filtered through this light sort of unconsciousness?

Rosemyn is delighted with her second visit, and I promise she can stay extra long — an hour! But after thirty short minutes, Roland arrives unexpectedly at the official visiting hour. I'm worn out and ask him quickly and cleverly to take Rose back to 6 East — saves me ringing the bell and waiting, saves two nurses the trip. . . .

Although I can see Rose's bewilderment, I don't react to it. I use the time Roland's away to catch my breath.

It could have been simple: *Hi, Roland. Give Rose and me a few minutes to say good-bye. Find out if there's coffee.*

Why don't I do what is simple?

Roland represents my colleagues and students, so for a moment I'm back in society, part of the outer world, which is stimulating.

At about eight p.m. I try to phone Rosemyn. A busy signal. Just to make sure, I dial again, and now she answers instantly.

"Hey," I exclaim, "the line was busy a second ago!"

"I was calling you," she says.

"Both at the same time!"

"Why did *you* call?"

"Because I blundered when we said good-bye."

"Yes."

"It was too quick, wasn't it? I did it all wrong. And I'm sorry."

She can only cry.

I say, "Let's make a new start tomorrow."

"Now!"

"No, I'm so tired I can't talk. Next time I'll ask visitors to wait outside, OK?"

"For a long time."

"All right. Good night for now?"

"G'night."

"It's great that you can use the phone. Do other children get that special treatment?"

"No."

Other children have a father or mother who comes and stays with them.

Nurse Erwin is with her.

She says, "It's too soon for Mam to die. It's not fair."

She's afraid of tomorrow's X-ray and conceals the pain in her elbow — let sleeping dogs lie.

After a while, Rosemyn indicated she wanted to sleep. And she did.

Tonight your closest friends have gathered at Catherine's, and the concentration of their love will do you good. Some of them feel so much happiness about your radiance (which I experienced myself yesterday) that Trudy reminds them of the sadness, which she knows so well.

Mia brings up the point that our wish to keep you here mustn't stand in your way, blocking your freedom of choice. We can only carry you to the light (in either direction), where a decision will follow of its own accord.

Wednesday, December 23rd

Phoebe's had a good night, but at five-thirty she's cold and is given an extra blanket. Rosemyn gets one too. Why do they have to grow cold first? It's December, damn it, and they're ill!

Rose woke at four from the pain in her arm. Or from nerves? She talks about you, is very sad, but says that she can turn to me. And this confirmation is so important, especially after last night's failure.

While nurse Janet is reading to her, Rosemyn suddenly says, "Are your hips hurting?"

"How do you know?"

"I can just see it."

Janet has a hip problem and isn't comfortable sitting on the stool, but she's never mentioned it.

After a cup of hot milk, I sleep till three a.m. myself, then lie awake in low spirits for an hour before ringing to ask for another Seresta. The nurse doesn't like the idea, but she can't calm me down, so she checks with the resident and brings me a lower dose.

Phoebe asks for a slice of bread and eats it with relish. I'd never have thought that bread could give so much joy. She begins to take an interest in her surroundings, including the toys, and she talks with Rosemyn and the staff.

All this so shortly after her visit to me, with the brutal honesty about you! Does it prove that openness is best? Or simply necessary? And she may have felt deep down that I'm here now, getting better — not just physically. Could this be drawing her back to earth?

She enjoys a bath, until the shampoo, after which she's exhausted and agitated. Her first bath and already a shampoo — *why?* It's happened before I know anything about it, before I can explain with how much patience and subtlety you did that.

Sleep has offered Phe safety by the time Joan comes to play her music. What a mercy to recover to the sounds of a lyre. But while Joan is playing, the room is cleaned. Couldn't that wait? Phe wakes up, but she doesn't turn away from Joan, as she did before; she lies on her back and listens.

Joan prepares for these moments thoroughly, even asks a teacher for advice ("Play a lot of quints — no songs"), and fortunately the nurses notice the soothing, healing effect of the music.

A few weeks ago, Joan asked permission to play here as a student. Permission was denied. And now she's been invited through a different channel.

Phoebe wants to say something, but she can't find the right words: "I must think. . . . I know it, but I can't say it."

Once again she's removed the stomach tube. But a new one isn't inserted because she's eaten. She's also gotten rid of the thermometer.

Visitors are still shocked when they see her, though. Her left eye is half shut, and when she turns her head, the whole upper part of her body moves along with it. Any kind of paper she gets hold of — newspapers, postcards, sheets of drawing paper — she tears up quietly. Even the dolls she's had all her life are not safe in her hands.

She's chronically overtired, and here on the other side of the building I'm anxious about the bustle in that room, created enthusiastically by Rosemyn. I'm telling myself:

Never mind. It's perfect — this will get Phe back on earth. It's exactly what she needs, a natural process. . . . She won't benefit from too much concern. Perhaps it's just my own fatigue that's bothering me.

Both Rose and Phe love being read to. Their cousins read for hours, almost every afternoon, so that I can enjoy private chats with Lauren. The way these teenagers do this is remarkable. At twelve, fourteen, and seventeen, you don't exactly share the world of smaller children.

For all of the past week, Lauren got diarrhea the minute she entered the hospital; that's how deeply the night of the crash affected her. People may have a lot of admiration for *me,* but standing by and looking on must be just as hard. By sharing, some people have literally taken on some of the suffering, decreasing ours.

This afternoon Rosemyn is taken out of traction, and I presume her exuberance of the past few days has had something to do with that. She's already hinted at a surprise: She'll come *walking* into my room.

I'm looking forward to it, but with mixed feelings, because when Rose can walk, she'll be discharged. Mam and Dad have offered to come and stay in our house, but then my own daughter would become even more of a visitor. And what would Phe do without her big sister, the complementary extravert?

As a matter of fact, I'm the first to be on my feet again, if one may call it that: leaning on a walker, which usually old people shuffle around with.

Drip and catheter have been removed almost without my notice; they belong to the distant past already. And actually, I've no idea when the oxygen tube was taken out!

I'm pleased with my four aluminum legs, and I'm very proud of myself — shaky and dizzy, but ever so proud! Mam and Dad are in the first row of the grandstand, and here I go, strutting around the corner of my bed . . . and falling flat on my face if that alert physical therapist hadn't reacted so quickly.

Let's regard it as a lesson in humbleness.

On behalf of all your friends, I call Doctor Lohmann again. Should treatment be ended, we'd like to be informed, so that friends and relatives can be there with flowers and music. She will let me know, of course, but she'll need to confer about the flowers and music. Again I'm struck by her commitment and understanding. But . . . She's not prolonging your life unnecessarily, is she?

The small things of life still continue. I get a potty chair on wheels that feels like a Rolls to me. With the help of my walker or the supportive arms of a nurse, I can manage to sit on the chair in front of the washstand to pee, and also to wash very slowly, leaning on the stand, while nurse Geoff is doing my back. I'm afraid to look in the mirror: I don't want to know how visitors see me.

After Rose is taken out of traction, a nurse writes: *Rosemyn was moved, had misty eyes, but was brave.*

She gets a different bed and sits upright a bit.

This is yet another incident that I only hear about. I wonder if the misty eyes were about emotion or pain. In the released elbow is a deep cut where the edge of the bandage was. It's treated with ointment now, but shouldn't it have been prevented?

Annet's report: *Rosemyn is quite wayward and a little cheeky, especially when more people are around. She's a child who needs a lot of rules and structure (also in her father's opinion). It's partly a pose; when I'm alone with her, it's all different; then I get through to her much better.*

What luck that Annet has the time and interest to do that.

You were often the only one who could reach Rose mentally when she was lost in a group of people. And whether I'll be able to succeed you in this . . .

At bedtime her arm still hurts, and she has trouble finding a comfortable position. She speaks little about you but would like to phone me.

I can't really comfort her tonight. There's general confusion and dismay about your condition. Bacteria have accumulated on the inside of your lungs. One of your pupils is fixed, which means that in half of your brain there's no activity at all. In fact, you've been brain dead for a while now.

However, when your parents tell me they know three people who were in a coma much longer and are up and about again, doing everything, hope has got me in its clutches all over again.

Would we truly be able to cope without you? Is it our

fear that's blocking your way out? Do you want *us* to let go? Take action?

You're braver than we are.

Catherine gives me a tape recorder with an empty tape so that I can talk to you and convey at least *something* of myself. But do we want another machine for this? We'll talk inwardly more often.

Or am I being a coward? Because I don't know what to say? Certainly not out loud!

OK, I will try.

I wait until late in the evening, when nobody will interrupt, but I can tell my voice won't hold out. As soon as I'm beginning to say how much I love you and your decision will be the right one and we'll manage, the three of us, I can only cry uncontrollably.

The second I stop feeling guilty about that, I have an idea. Remember when I bought Brahms's *Piano Pieces* for my mam's birthday? In the store I listened to the first piece and was touched by the old folk-song that inspired Brahms:

> *Sleep well, my child,*
> *sleep softly and well.*
> *It hurts me so*
> *to see you cry.*

There's a parallel with the lines in Handel's *St. John's Passion*, which I was struck by years ago, almost as if I had a premonition of now:

80

Slumber now, Thy toil is ended.
Softly rest, Thy task is done.

The music can speak for me.
What else can I do but be honest?
Please, may rest come soon for you.

Thursday, December 24th

Phoebe is agitated again, and they take her to another room. She's scared of the bell button and normally wakes Rosemyn to ring it, who helps out eagerly. What will she do in the other room?

After having been read to, she sleeps well and is woken at a quarter past eight. Why don't they let her sleep? *My* nurses break the routine and skip taking my temperature until later.

Phoebe eats and drinks, has a bath at her own request (her hair is washed too), and plays with her dolls! In my room, at coffee time, she drinks from the delicious juices that were thoughtful presents, grabs a piece of cake from my hands — "Can I eat? I want it" — and swallows it in one go. She protests when she has to leave.

Rosemyn is taken for an X-ray by bed. When they suddenly lift her up and sit her on a stool for the X-ray (just like that, after she's been in traction for ten days), she vomits.

Back in the ward, she can walk a few steps. That goes well! Her arm is very painful, though.

Nurses' report: *Sometimes Rosemyn is a nuisance. When we're busy with Phoebe, she interferes all the time.*

They must be desperate: how does one handle a girl who's equally sad and difficult? Doctors, nurses, dietary assistants, all kinds of therapists . . . They spend a lot of time on us that they don't really have.

Rosemyn wants to go home — that is, "To Gran and Granddad," she tells people, "because my father's in the hospital."

While she's walking around, the X-ray comes back, and it's bad news: the bone hasn't healed, and she'll have to be in traction for ten more days. That's very unusual indeed; the bed's already been replaced by a regular one.

The new traction can wait until tonight, and here she comes walking into my room after all.

"Hi, Dad!"

The expression on her face is a mixture of toughness and disillusionment; she's only too conscious of this empty surprise. But since I've been told about the X-ray, I *am* surprised by her coming and show my joy over a-whole-day-out-of-traction, so that she does have a good time. At last we can hug — careful! — and feel what will some day be real again.

Nestling softly against me, she asks, "Which is your sore leg again?" And, "When will your lungs be better?"

I'll soon be able to ride in a wheelchair to 6 East.

Is it fate that's arranged to keep her here with Phe and me?

In the lounges of several wards, a choir of volunteers are singing carols. It's the halting, improvised character that moves me. Now it feels as if the other performance by the Salvation Army group was months ago. Sometimes it's encouraging to look back and compare.

So it will be Christmas.

That's a celebration, but even in the old days, some carols made me feel gloomy. (The wrong music or the wrong me?)

Somehow, hearing the voices in the distance, it's just as if I'm among the people of two thousand years ago, leaving their houses or tents to feel the coming of Christ in the middle of a plain, under the stars.

Some songs move me so, it hurts.

In her ward, Phoebe goes and listens with Rianne.

Rosemyn is having a bath, using the opportunity of her arm being free, and Ann takes over the hairwashing from a nurse, but you know how Rose can bridge a distance with all her senses!

Nurse's report: *Rosemyn liked the choir very much, sang a song that was/is her mother's favorite.*

You need to have your chest drained because one of your

lungs has collapsed. This can't save the lung, but it will relieve you.

Your body suffers badly. The permanent lying in bed causes bruising. Tubes have torn the corners of your mouth. More and more mucus has to be drained from your bronchi. Still, miracles happen all the time, so why not for you like for us? Some people are vexed when we talk about your dying. At times it's all so contradictory.

It's Christmas Eve.

Phoebe is strangely out of sorts. She undresses completely and wets her bed twice. She won't let her temperature be taken.

Nurse's report: *Rosemyn said her mother was much better.*

And thanks to the draining, you are — in some respects.

She's back in traction but lying wrong: an extra rail is needed for the pulleys. She's upset, keeps ringing for small things and won't sleep. According to the nurses' reports, she was upset by the fuss with the traction.

"I've made a little prayer: 'Dear Mam, when you're going to die, please tell me. Then I'll tell Dad.'"

Or does she mean "if"? (In Dutch, there's one word for "when" and "if," and I didn't ask which she meant.)

Among the friends who visit you regularly, a turmoil has been caused by the question of whether I can and want or ought to go to see you. This is both important and difficult, even for those who are used to dealing with meta-physical matters. Out of respect, they don't want to interfere. Not knowing what's going on between you and me, they can't yet grasp what's happening in a spiritual dimension.

For days Annicka has felt some pressure about whether or not to ask me about seeing you. She shares absolutely everything with you, doesn't she? You have a telepathic bond, and this afternoon at your bedside she asks you the question that's bothered everyone for so long now: "Dear Marian, what is it you're waiting for?"

The answer she receives without words: *For Arno.*

The rest of the day, this weighs on her heavily. Feeling like a coward, she yields to the general hesitation and silent command to leave me in peace. It's the ultimate test of the inner voice. When I happen to phone her myself (about a small practical matter I could have asked anyone else), she feels compelled to speak and chooses the way of a question: "Are you going to see Marian?"

I think of what Geoff has offered a few times.

Don't they understand that I have no choice?

Or am I the one who's a coward?

I perspire continuously and run a temperature. I spend all my energy, including my reserves, on the children. After using the bathroom, I can just barely recover before a doctor, the physical therapist, Rosemyn, or Phoebe arrives. Mail, phone calls, and "resting" come somewhere in between. When the girls are here, I show them that I'm strong and that everything will be fine. How long would it take me to recover from a trip to Denton?

No, you don't need my justification, do you?

Or am I clinging to excuses? Maybe Rose and Phe would gladly do without me for even a few days if that enabled me to visit you, happy with that proof of courage and manliness.

Annicka's story is a challenge to my intuition: Which feeling is the most sincere and vital one? The girls come first and foremost with you, but you're suffering, you're lonely, longing for the freedom you've shown me. Perhaps you need to have me with you just once. . . .

But here I am! *Feel* me. All I do is in the name of you!

Or . . .

Shall I come and touch you?

I'm afraid you'd feel my grief and helplessness, with nothing to give.

I love you so.

To avoid drowning in the Sea of Galilee, Peter "only" needs to *trust*.

Annicka functions like deep water, to make me feel the deepest in myself and find the resources there. What a task for her. . . . She's convinced that you need me in Denton because there are moments you can't bear the loneliness. She tells me about the question she asked you and how much it costs her to say this, fearing the loss of our friendship.

It's true: I'm furious.

By the way, the gemstone she gave me the other day is gone. I've searched the mess on my table and in the drawers twice.

I don't doubt the authenticity of either your answer or Annicka's interpretation, and I know she spoke out of concern for you; otherwise, it wouldn't be so alarming. But I feel undermined, as if she's driving a wedge between you and me.

Poor Annicka! Losing you, her best friend, caring and standing by in two hospitals, looking after three sons on her own. . . .

The curious thing is that in spite of my anger, I don't feel any grudge against her. Somehow she must be a link, an extremely important one, in something much larger, which I'll understand one day.

In order to find out what I'll be capable of toward you, what kind of bond we really have, I'll need to consult an unknown part of myself and be utterly honest. This has to do with trust, and it's the most difficult and most beautiful thing there is.

Raymond and Marjorie bring yellow roses with an exquisite scent. Since they have their own children, family, and friends, making it hard to join in even their everyday lives, it's extra-special to have them here on Christmas Eve.

"We had an appointment for this afternoon, remember?" Raymond says. "Only now we're coming to you."

I tell them about the conflict between Annicka and me, and again he suggests, "Would you like to ask Marian herself?"

They'll help me with their own meditations.

This time I close my eyes.

I do the "exercise," ask my question timidly, and see you as an ancient goddess or priestess or pharaoh's daughter. Some time ago you had this kind of square, straight haircut. I remember the famous pictures in art and history books, but this is you.

Your wonderful eyes are closed, relaxed, but not in sleep. It's supreme concentration, pure sublimity, and your beauty is of such sacredness that I'm afraid to look at you.

You're either performing or being taught a difficult task; I'd better not intrude. Yet I ask, "Can I do something for you?"

The image disappears.

I try to go back to your field on the high coast, but the contact is now obscured by sentimentality: hand in hand we descend to a pond where Rosemyn and Phoebe are playing. No, this is my own wishful thinking, not a picture of your situation.

The stillness of the Egyptian vision returns, and I think: How did I dare ask that question! You're so magnificent and so deeply engaged in something crucial — compared to that, my lessons are easy.

If I can't do anything specific for you, I'll continue the way I was doing things.

Raymond and Marjorie were each made to think of "lesson" too, and they're just as impressed with your greatness as I am.

Raymond asked, "Do you experience anything of Christmas?" He felt alerted to his stupidity when you said, "It's always Christmas here."

Friday, December 25th

Rosemyn and Phoebe have slept well, although the skin of Rosemyn's elbow hurts under the sticking plaster. Ten more days. Another bandage is added to stop her fiddling with it. It's not cutting into the same spot, is it?

All three of us, though in separate wings, enjoy the breakfast of fancy rolls, Christmas loaf, boiled eggs, tea, and *jus d'orange.* Christmas doesn't have any significance yet, because the value of the days is defined by the messages about you and by the progress of our convalescence. But it's wonderful that we *can* enjoy this meal.

The morning brings a new phase and highlight: Mam and Dad take me in a wheelchair to see the girls at coffee time. It's a festive adventure; I feel like a film star.

They're in the playroom. Some pop music is playing loudly, and Phoebe looks a bit lost. Or is this *my* disappointment? After twelve days, I would have liked to meet them in their own room.

When we finally get there, where so many people have been before me, I find confusion about food requests: Phoebe is given milk, and Rosemyn is not, even though calcium is needed for her broken bone, and milk would be an easy contribution to the "six glasses of liquid a day" she has trouble with.

I've been so far away! Did I "just" mix up their names? Anyhow, I'm mad (what if Phe's allergy to milk will cause bronchitis again?), and the nurse gets mad at me.

OK, the staff can do without a worried, meddlesome father, so let's concentrate on solving the misunderstandings. At least I'm here now. Let's celebrate!

Coffee with Christmas cake! We're relishing the treat and the peace, praising this beautiful room. How good we have it here, and how well the three patients are doing.

The joy I feel because I can finally come to the girls — it's the first time we're all together — is stronger now than fear or sadness. Rosemyn is in a glowing mood. It's quite awhile before I've admired all their mail, drawings, presents, games, and candy.

Right across the room, the sun is shining on the thrones of their beds, adorned with the photos of you. How striking: after weeks and weeks of the dullest, darkest weather, it's a very sunny day.

In my wheelchair I can ride to the windows and enjoy the view. It's so light in here, it hurts my eyes.

"Your room is facing south!"

"No, it's 6 East."

"That's the wing itself, but this side of it is south."

I can see the countryside, with tiny roads and cars. No sounds come in from outside, as if we don't belong to that world.

I hurry from one daughter to the other; there's so much to be shared!

"Have you got a Christmas tree?" Rosemyn asks my mam and dad.

"Yes. And for you we've brought some pastry rings. . . ."

"Mmm, chocolate!"

"You've got heaps of sweets already, but today is special."

Somehow, in the course of this morning, there grows inside me the deepest sense of Christmas I've ever had — a quiet, universal kind of joy — although I scarcely dare say it and believe it.

Toward noon, before the meal, Mam and Dad wheel me back to my room. Since I insist, Dad eats the Florida cocktail and *bavarois* of fresh pineapple, while I'm sipping a soup flavored with red wine and served with dove, fine vegetables, and breadsticks.

After they've left, I have the fillet with a stuffing of turkey-mince, paprika, mushrooms, and truffles, doused with a light cream of sherry. Very consciously, I enjoy the savoriness and eat a bit more than I usually do — also the chicory with ham and cheese, bunch carrots, and potato cake — to "get strong" again.

Nurse's report: *Mr. B. looks very cheerful. Doesn't talk about the crash or the condition of his wife.*

Immediately after this, before the resting hour, Dr. Lohmann calls. She tells me your treatment will be terminated at five this afternoon. Your condition has suddenly worsened radically — and definitively.

I can't speak because I'm crying, or trying to put that off.

She's affected herself.

After a lovely morning, when *everything* seemed to end well . . .

You'll never come back.

Ah, Rose and Phe . . .

In a few hours' time.

All right. Of course it's all right, even if the blow is unexpected after all.

I'm happy for you. At last.

So that's what you've been waiting for: to witness my going to the children because I *want* to, not because I have to, so that you be sure we'll go on, the three of us (among many).

Dr. Lohmann was going away for the holidays, and your parents and Judy, torn between hoping and "knowing," asked her specifically if it made any sense to prolong your life until she came back. Even this morning, before the long drive to her in-laws, Judy hesitated and checked. "No news," she was told.

Dr. Lohmann will never be able to explain why all of a sudden this entire team of specialists met on Christmas Day (called back from private lives) and decided to stop your treatment.

"Absurd," she will say, looking back — also thinking of future Christmas Days.

But we know better: our happiness of this morning gave you the final courage to say good-bye. It was like a symbolic step I took toward the children.

If, apart from this, you did need me beside you physically . . .

Forgive me.

We won't know how you'll be doing from now on. We'll never see or hear you again. You are really leaving. There won't be any new memories of you in our lives. But how we'll miss you is not relevant now. This afternoon we'll be allowed to bring you flowers, music, and candles. I'll make some phone calls. With Rosemyn and Phoebe, I'll be close inwardly. I'll do my best and stand by.

Action is called for. Work and grief are divided. I call Mam and Dad, Lauren and friends, who'll phone the others.

Christmas dinners are canceled. Children are taken to stay with friends or neighbors who didn't know you, who have their own families visiting. With whom can death be shared on this day celebrating birth?

Lauren will be here in a minute. Annicka's just left for a few days on the coast, and Trudy tries to reach her there.

Dad will give you the Old Testament priest's blessing.

Since the stores are closed, I ask him on the phone, "Have you got suitable flowers to take?"

"No," he says, "*you* have beautiful flowers. I'll come and get them."

Lauren and her children bring a pine branch with Christmas pastry rings to Rosemyn and Phoebe.

True, it's still Christmas. Birth, death, redemption. And let's be fair: Christmas is meant to remind us of something that has its effect somewhere every day.

Through the windows on the corridor side, they can see that Rosemyn is taking her nap. The door is closed.

They wait and think about what to do. Then, in her sleep, she says clearly, "Mammy, Mam . . ."

In your own way, in this deeper kind of awareness of which sleep is only a moment, only one layer, you're letting her know you're going on.

And Phoebe . . . She must have been close to you permanently, saying good-bye all this time.

Although my room is full of flowers, it goes without saying that I'll send along the fragrant roses. They've just opened: a deep, warm yellow.

With Lauren, I think out loud: There are ten of them, but for some reason we like nine better. Or should it be three, one from each of us? Or four, since you still belong? And sometimes you gave somebody just one, which is now meaningful too.

"Nine is three times three," Lauren says. "The number of completeness. And the one you'd keep is another beginning."

Yes. I needn't think about it any longer.

We needn't choose, either: one rose turns out to be limp — broken, really. I ask Lauren to cut it very short, although it seems past saving, and find a small, pretty vase for it.

With the utmost care, Dad wraps your bunch of flowers in a pile of newspapers for their trip through the frost — this first, crystalline, purifying frost.

Leon, Elise, and Rachel are still in 6 East, and suddenly I grow aware of what I've felt for a while: Hurry to

Rosemyn and Phoebe yourself! The phone calls, the roses, and the unexpected, unsuspecting visitors bringing chocolates and flowers have distracted me from what needs to be conquered. What's come over me — to leave three "children" with Rose and Phe, knowing all this time you're about to die? Their inner conflict must be agony.

The moment Lauren wheels me into their room, all of that is visible. Phoebe looks around unaware, with her perpetual smile, but Rosemyn is in tears from attempts to understand and be good. Her eyes are black.

"Oh, my girl, do you know?"

"How's Mam?" she asks.

At lunchtime they tucked away French fries. After that, it says in the nurse's report, *Rosemyn was very noisy: screaming, calling names . . .*

Mainly Leon, her big, strong, adored cousin — the brother in her dreams — has been a target. Or rather, a shield for her anger at you, the one who's leaving her behind.

If only her cousins had *said* what they knew.

But how could I expect them to?

Later she'll want a moment with Leon, to apologize.

"The doctor called," I tell her. "Your mam's condition is so bad that the treatment will be stopped."

"And then?"

"She can finally die."

"*Why?*"

"Perhaps she's going to have an important, special task in heaven. She's already been special to us, and now she knows, I think, that we'll make it together. I'm happy for her, that she can have a rest."

A bed used for teenagers is fetched for me, because I won't be able to sit much longer. I end up lying on my back between the girls' beds.

In the meantime, before Lauren goes home, she waters the flowers in my room and puts the yellow rose on my bedside table, although it's still drooping.

I'm too tired to talk. Besides, we want to maintain contact with you more than ever. We listen to Monteverdi's *Vespers* — the concert you and I went to. With outstretched arms I'm holding the children's hands, so I can't wipe away my tears. Rosemyn sees them.

Then it is silent.

There's not much left to do but look upward.

Is it still the same day as this morning, when I was here for the first time?

Phoebe seems to be asleep.

Rosemyn turns more or less out of traction to get some sheets of paper lying on the windowsill: song sheets of the carols that were sung by the choir yesterday. Groping for tone and words, she begins to sing. I have trouble finding the words too, and my voice is gone, but I can hum or whisper along.

As soon as there's a pause, when Rosemyn is thinking or leafing through song sheets, Phoebe mutters on my left, "Sing."

They're mostly classical carols but include "A Flower Is Springing." I wonder: Why does it have that corny reputation? It's just beautiful!

The clock in the corridor catches my eye. It's almost five when we're singing this.

Please, don't linger. Medically speaking, it could take a while — hard for those who are there with you — but no one expects that.

Right after we've finished singing, Dad's on the phone in the office, and a nurse takes me there.

You've died instantly.

You'd reached the limits of your strength.

Again, I'm unable to speak.

He's quiet, letting me cry.

The nurse comes back and asks if I'm all right. She hands me some tissues and sees that I need to be alone for a while. At the same time, I'm relieved about your being free and the clearness of the situation — a new start. I shouldn't keep Rose and Phe waiting.

I still can't fathom how much Phoebe understands. So far, I've tried to discuss difficult issues as straightforwardly as possible, but to her I find it impossible to say, "Mam is dead." And she doesn't know the other, euphemistic or friendlier words. She lies motionless, her eyes closed, struggling with consciousness, so I sit by Rosemyn's side. (Their beds are not far away from each other.)

We don't lower our voices; we're not shutting Phoebe out. She's close enough: let her take in what she wants from a distance, as gradually as necessary.

"Is Mam happy now?" Rosemyn asks.

"Yes."

"Doesn't she miss us?"

"No, *heaven* means there's no such thing as 'missing

someone.' Mam has no sense of time now. To her, past and present aren't anything separate."

Out of the celestial blue, Rosemyn says absent-mindedly, "We don't need my prayer anymore. I've thought of something else. Can I say it?"

"Of course."

"Have you ever looked into heaven?
Perhaps if you look hard,
you will see an angel who is new —
and that is my Mam."

I ask her to say it again, so that I can write it down. My zeal and emotion do her good. We're both very happy with it, and I read it to Phoebe.

The nurses suggest I stay here for the night, and they don't understand why I decline. I can't explain how much I need *my* nurses, my potty chair, the button to lower or raise the back support of my bed, and the opportunity to choose to keep silent or talk freely about you, the girls, and myself. I can't explain how I accept their loneliness.

I go back to my room.

Thea and Mia tell me about your final hours in the physical world.

In addition to your parents, Judy, and my dad, seven women are present. They fill the room with love and flowers, gathered from everywhere (on this holiday): train-station shops, gardens, their own or friends' homes. . . .

There's been a short deliberation about which to hear first: the Word or the music?

Dad says, "I would choose the music first, but knowing Marian and Arno, that should come last."

His hand on your head, he gives you the ancient blessing, not in the usual subjunctive mood, but like this:

"The Lord blesses you and keeps you.

The Lord makes his face to shine upon you, and is gracious to you.

The Lord lifts up his countenance upon you, and gives you peace."

Elisabeth plays "A Flower Is Springing." She's brought a lot of musical scores but chooses this at the last moment, partly because it's simple, which helps her control her nervousness. I didn't even know she was going to play at all, so it's a remarkable, wonderful "coincidence."

A circle is formed around you, and roses are laid beside your head.

Your mother gives you a kiss — "Good-bye, my child . . ." — and caresses your face.

She has a strength and an acceptance that rise far above the usual, which has an effect on everyone.

Nobody cries.

They have to leave you for a while, during the technical, unpleasant procedure, but they stay nearby and carry you to the light.

At last, the tubes and machines are gone.

Your hair seems to be golden again. Or it's the way these friends can see you, now as always.

A tape of music is left to play when they leave: Slovenian liturgies of beyond time.

Thea gives me the honey candle that's just been burned for you. It has a strong, lovely scent. The wax has solidified and will melt again here.

When she's about to leave my room, Mia hesitates. "Is there anything we can do for you?"

There's something about the way she asks it that makes me think thoroughly. But no, I only need some rest, to take in quietly what I did and did not attend.

Mia has her hand on the doorknob but comes back. She'll have to say what they came for. "Have you thought of . . . Where would you like Marian's body to be taken?"

She's afraid to obtrude and bring up these worries now.

I have been thinking about that, but I only got as far as the wish: Could you go home for a while?

There is no home.

I wouldn't be there for you.

"We'd like to bring her to your house," Mia says. "There are enough people to stay with her in turns. For days and nights too."

What a gift.

The loneliness surrounding death is something I've always been frightened of. Years ago, we talked about both the intimate matters and the practical bother — insurance, funeral "service." . . . I remember asking Geraldine, "Would you be able to sing at the funeral of a friend?"

We were fascinated by the control and expression of emotion that a singer has.

"I truly don't know," she said. "I'd *want* to, but whether my voice would hold out . . ."

Now Mia goes on. "Trudy knows somebody who takes good care of the official side of it all. He's got a great deal of experience with unusual situations, and he's a sensitive person."

The word "undertaker" hasn't crossed my mind yet.

After I've told them how grateful I am, they're just as relieved themselves. Maybe they thought we had arranged this long ago.

Mr. Timmons arrives half an hour later with a list of questions that require sober thinking. Burial or cremation? What kind of coffin? Black or blue suits for the bearers?

"Thought so," he often says after my answers, which is very reassuring, because we've never made any decisions about these things, just thought and talked about them in the abstract.

Rosemyn wants to see you, and tentatively I ask Timmons, "Could Marian be brought to us here in the hospital — on her way home?"

It would be painfully characteristic if you were the one to make this last step toward us.

"As for transport," he says, "I'll try my best, but tomorrow is Boxing Day. Besides, we'd need permission from the hospital."

We look at each other and realize only too well that this has never been done before.

"At least we can ask. . . ."

The directors? On Christmas?

I even ask if you may stay in my room for a day.

Timmons sets to work.

It takes a while for my nurse to see what I mean. Then she phones the head nurse, who phones a director. My room is too small, and it's at the far end of the wing. But 548, which is closer to the elevators and much larger, happens to be vacant (because it's the holidays?) and is put at our disposal, provided everything will be over before visiting hours.

Timmons phones to say that transport can be arranged, but there's a problem: the authorities have "claimed" your body because you've died within thirty days after the accident. A coroner will have to establish the cause of death independently before your body can be released.

As if you are a car!

Of course these are routine formalities. But nobody knows when this doctor will come or how long the assessment will take. Only after that can your body be tended to, and then the journey here and our good-byes will have to take place before two o'clock, the beginning of visiting hours.

Again my faith is tested, because bureaucracy is by definition impenetrable: we can't phone anyone or ask the doctor to come early. Although I know you're far away already, it's terrible to think your body may have to stay in a cold, impersonal room.

In the meantime, I must decide about the clothes

you'll wear. What comes to mind first is your old, hand-made outfit: the golden brown sweater and skirt. We've all seen you in it so often, and you were fabulous in it. But I don't dare resolve this on my own, so I call Lauren, who has the same idea right away, even though there are many possibilities, like the brand-new ensemble that was a present from your parents.

Trish will go and get the skirt and sweater, as well as a blouse, and take them to Timmons's tonight.

How brave, to go through your clothes in the deserted house.

My mam has some thoughts about a good-bye "service" at home, and I think they suit you and the situation very well. Although there was something inscrutable about you (some call it "carefulness"), many people appear to know you through and through.

Conrad offers to take photos in case we won't be able to be there.

No, please don't. That would feel like a desecration, especially of the moment you'll be leaving the house.

Rosemyn is restless and emotional, worrying about Phoebe. She doesn't fall asleep until half past nine and keeps waking up.

Mia gets in a panic about her offer. You and she didn't share everyday life — your friendship was an undercurrent — and she doesn't know our other friends well enough to organize the vigil for day and night. She calls

Trudy, who's been through this, although with Hanny it was arranged *for* them.

I remember that you left in the middle of the night to be with Hanny for an hour, and how still you were in response to my clumsy questions the next day.

What I *don't* remember is whether I got up on time in the morning to let you sleep.

There was much I wouldn't let myself be touched by — mainly things like pain, loneliness, sacrifice, and death. I never went through them, so I didn't find out what is behind them.

Trudy is on the phone for hours, inviting the right people for the vigil and giving them some necessary explanations, the delicacy of which is embedded in practical details. She organizes the twelve night-time hours and asks me to do the same for daytime.

A number of friends are still away, in some cases to recover from grief and fatigue. Single parents who'd like to be with you have to appeal for help in order to take their turns. But I find that all of them, in every strand of the web of support, want to take part in this, as if they want to come and feel something of you that will last for the rest of their lives.

Tomorrow afternoon, Mia and Thea will receive you in our house.

Saturday, December 26th

The seemingly dead rose in the little vase on my table has fully straightened up and is opening. The scent and warmth of its yellow fill the room as strongly as the whole bunch did — but in a different way.

Although this touches me as a token of you, I'm still worrying about your body: What kind of room is it in now? How will it be handled? Please, let them be on time!

Rosemyn has been told I'll be with her at eight-thirty this morning, to talk about our saying good-bye. But after breakfast, toilet — bathing skipped — and "the journey" from my wing to hers, it's nine o'clock. These thirty minutes have seemed long to her and no doubt to the nurses too.

Rosemyn was disappointed in Dad. We met him in the corridor, and we discussed the procedure for today. He soon focused on the practical things of life: eating and drinking habits of the children. Dad was approached positively, and some clear agreements were made; the dietitian is informed. We asked Dad to stick to the agreements for Rosemyn's sake, for clarity and confidence. Dad talks with Rosemyn in a rather grown-up way and always confers with her before a decision can be made.

I feel like a schoolkid called to the principal's office: so much admonishment before I'm allowed to see Rosemyn.

She loved her first glass of hot milk and honey, so the six glasses of liquid a day won't be a problem anymore. It's great that I can finally come and see to this myself.

Sitting unwashed in my wheelchair, I remember the care you took over the girls' meals.

Two nurses advise me to bring Phoebe to you as well. Although she doesn't even know about the crash or your death, I agree that would be a wise thing to do, even if it's frightening.

In the course of this morning comes the news that in Denton everything went well. Towards one o'clock, you're expected here at 5 West.

It sounds like a distinguished visit, and that's what it is. The staff of all wings on this floor are informed of it, to prevent mobile patients from being caught by surprise — by seeing a coffin. The nurses are busy preparing your room, using the yellow cubicle curtains to make a private corner. From my room, the most beautiful postcards and about fifteen bouquets are moved to 548, and dozens of tea-light candles are gathered from several wards.

I'm trying to talk about "your body" instead of "you," but that doesn't feel good: we haven't said good-bye yet.

You're here, after all this time of inward contact.

First I go in alone, although I need to be wheeled to

the coffin. The atmosphere is created by the sunlight, enhanced by the flowers, candles, and curtains. This makes the shock caused by death itself that much worse. What I see has nothing to do with you anymore. After the many stories about your ethereal radiance, even amid the machines . . .

Your face is swollen and bluish. Your dazzling eyes can't show anything. The corners of your mouth are sagging and bloodstained. Even your hands, lying folded on your sweater, are swollen. My darling, what have they done to you?

What a sacrifice to travel a roundabout way, enduring the rough journey when you need nothing but peace.

Then I see the necklace of shells: it looks so natural on you. Well done, Trish. I hadn't thought of any jewelry at all.

Shells — your hands picking them up, the pensive way you kneel in the sand, one with the elements. . . . They help me feel your inner self again.

I caress your forehead and hands.

Cold. Insensible.

I've never seen a dead person before.

You're dead. I can see it. We don't feel each other any longer.

How long will I have to stay here to make that sink in?

We still have the girls together. They're waiting. And now comes despair. Is this right for children of six and nine? Wouldn't this picture of you dominate the rest of their lives? On the other hand, it would be even more difficult if a picture were missing.

Back in my room, where Mam and Lauren are waiting, I say plainly, "I need your help. Please, go and see if this is too hard for the girls."

Would it be a mental cruelty?

Then, oddly enough, as soon as they've left, I know what needs to be done: I'll tell Rosemyn exactly what happened to me just now, and she'll decide for herself what to do. As for Phoebe, suddenly I believe that will solve itself too.

So again, even *asking* for help may suffice.

Coming back, Mam says, also in tears, "This is the most difficult question of my life."

Still, I feel extraordinary peace, underneath.

"Mam's body has become very ugly," I tell Rosemyn. "It's awful to see. Are you sure you want to go?"

She nods without a trace of hesitation.

I ask Phoebe, "Do you want to come with us? To say good-bye to Mam?"

Smiling, she says, "Yes."

I still think *accident* and *death* haven't gotten through to her. These are words of the earth, and she hasn't really returned yet.

I'm holding her on my lap in the wheelchair; Rose is in her bed. Two nurses take us to 5 West, where more staff are waiting. They have an anxious expression on their faces.

We're put beside your coffin. The staff withdraw.

Rosemyn can't see well, is on the wrong side, wriggling dangerously, trying to see you over her right shoulder. Phoebe is too low on my knees, since the coffin is high on a cooling device. Their nurses, watching from a distance, decide to take Rose out of traction. Held in their arms, she observes you thoroughly. "Not ugly at all — it's really still Mam. Only some blood. Why has Mam got blood on her mouth?"

Phoebe notices there's something in the coffin and indicates clearly that she wants to see what we're looking at so intensely. She's lifted onto the foot of her bed, which was brought along empty, and she too gets the opportunity to face your death.

"Mam's asleep," she says.

I'm surprised she's recognized you.

"Yes," I say, "Mam's dead. This is Mam's dead body."

Rosemyn is stroking your face.

I'm ashamed of my surprise. They're not put off by your outside: they're looking straight through it.

When we're taken out, Timmons is waiting by the door. What wonderful work he's done! At the same time, Ernest and Nicky arrive, and what moves me is the way they're dressed: in dark, sober clothing.

Back in my room, I'm numb, frozen, broken, absent.

Is this mental or emotional vacuum a kind of shield?

The children have to rest. The others don't want to leave, so they wait down in the hospital cafeteria. It's lunchtime, but they're not hungry.

Rosemyn can't sleep. The nurses realize she needs someone close to her, so they call the cafeteria.

Nicky and Ernest come up again. She gets into Rose's bed, and he, a bear of comfort, lies down beside Phe.

Nurse's report: *She didn't cry but is clearly impressed and reflects on it. She's coping with it in her shy and reticent way. This morning she didn't want to take a bath, which was all right, but then she smiled at that.*

As for eating, drinking, and urinating, it was easy to correct her today.

Phe's smile is always there. Just as if she thinks: That's how it's done, because everybody comes to me smiling.

My attention is so divided that the quality of it suffers: I should have been alone with Rosemyn all day, alone with Phoebe and with my family and myself. All of us really needed that. I don't even know how the children reacted afterwards.

It went well, I think — but is it something that *can* go well?

According to standard procedure, you'd be buried on Tuesday or Wednesday. Rosemyn will be allowed to go, with her arm in a weighted sling.

We've never been to a cemetery before. Rosemyn and Trudy have talked about Hanny's grave in Wornfield, and she would like you to be buried there too. I'm not sure about Gorsemere either, but at least I can do this for your parents and so for you, I hope. How much you loved the river there, with its forelands and swan sanctuary! How you played around the farms when you were little!

The same river runs past our house, where you'll be at home for a few more days.

From eight to eleven this morning, Trish and a friend cleaned the house from top to bottom, inside and outside. It's Trish's birthday tomorrow, but she won't celebrate. They're leaving for Highflow, where she'll cook a meal for two families because her mother is seriously ill.

Before she goes, she makes coffee for Mia and Thea, who will be staying with you all day, reviving your atmosphere.

Looking for objects that could help them, they find two sun-yellow sheets in Rosemyn's room to drape over your coffin. You dyed them yourself; the girls will soon be using them for tents and huts again.

Your parents come before your body has recovered from transport, and suddenly it's too much for them. Although I did fear your mother's heart was on the point of breaking, I'd asked them to be with you in the mornings, starting tomorrow, but they have to cancel that. Your mother has seen a cardiologist but hasn't told us yet. Did she know how bad it was?

Catherine brings thirty-eight very fresh roses, one of which turns out to be broken past saving. Yes, you wouldn't be thirty-eight until next month.

All of the flowers from Denton are still beautifully intact: daffodils, winter jasmine, a strongly fragrant hyacinth, and the roses. Candles are lit in the brass holders and in the Advent wreath you made. Music tapes are chosen carefully. The dollhouses, which you made for the girls with infinite love, are close to you.

Gradually, your radiance returns.

Just when it's weighing on me that I haven't found anyone for tonight's vigil yet, the phone rings: it's Eric, asking what he can do for me. I tell him, and he'd like to be with you tonight. The whole evening? Well, if he says he's pleased to do so, I mustn't doubt it.

Whom can I ask for early tomorrow morning (Sunday): neighbors who'll throw a coat over their pajamas and go back to bed afterwards?

"Bring a book or some needlework," I tell Gerald and Amy. "Make coffee or tea, play the music you like. . . . Please, take care that you feel at ease. Then Marian will be fine too."

"If we can do that for you," says Amy, "we will."

Although they're just as frightened as I used to be.

It takes courage to ask and receive in such quantities — a voyage of discovery for me.

Now I have a bit of time to think about a text for the mourning card. I want to convey both the cruelty of the crash and the essence of the metaphysical contact we've had. Rosemyn's "poem" is a gift that speaks for itself, so I'll begin with that, but how do I put the actual notification of your death into words for people who don't know anything about it yet? Many have been telephoned, but others will open the envelope unsuspectingly, thinking that it might contain a festive invitation. Because we don't want a black or gray edge on the envelopes, do we?

At five o'clock my meal is taken up to the girls' room. For Phoebe and me, a little table is put next to Rosemyn's bed. Somebody brings apples, peeled and cut into sections. Astonishing, how homey it's made here, and how much distress and weariness can be soothed by that.

Silently and slowly, Phoebe enjoys her slices of whole-meal bread. Then she says, "Mam is dead."

Again Rosemyn asks why, and again I tell her you're going onward, continuing the way you're meant to be going. I also tell her it's my turn to look after them now, but an angel can support a lot of people at the same time.

She's pondering. And I explain that we often don't know till later why something has happened to us.

Her arm has been bandaged again. She doesn't whine about the wound in the elbow fold. I wish she would. That would mean one less scar.

After supper, Trudy will read to them and rub their feet. To me, the intense moments they share before bed-time are only glimpses of their new existence.

Returned to 5 West, I'm caught by a loneliness that feeds on exhaustion. It's dark and chilly in my room. I feel like an outsider visiting himself. Better use the bathroom now, so I won't need to get out of bed anymore.

On my way back, I can feel a change in the room. The door is open, and a soft, warm light meets me in the corridor. A nurse has lit my candles.

It's Susan. She was eleven when her mother died, and her sister was nine. She tells me that her father wasn't sure whether to bring his daughters to the funeral. He did, but for her sister it was a traumatic event that she suffers from even now.

This releases me from an undermining dilemma.

Timmons and I are discussing the arrangements. Suddenly I ask, "Is there a *minimum* length of time required between the day of death and the funeral?"

"Yes. Thirty-six hours."

"So it could be Monday?"

"I think so."

"What could work against that?"

"Time for preparations, the mourning cards . . ."

"The cards could be sent afterwards. That would give us the peace we need for a quiet, personal farewell."

Should I consult anyone else? No, this is best. A wake of two days and nights is already a special expression of love.

An immense burden falls away. With all good-byes, it's the waiting that hurts the most. I'm sure this is what you want yourself. The exceptional concentration of energy of and for all these hard workers must have reached its peak and might soon be waning.

No one can tell how long we'll be here in the hospital; I ask Jack and Trish to bring more things from home. They look for music and games and find some medicines.

That was entirely your department. I don't know much about it and call Titia. She offers to go to you tomorrow and check the medicines.

There's always a phone call to be made or visitors and

doctors to be dealt with — between my trips to the children. As a result, the stitches in my leg haven't been removed yet. But only one nurse is worried about that.

I don't seem to take much time to think of you.

Perhaps I should call Catherine; if she could take over for Eric for half an hour, he'd be able to get here earlier, and I could go to sleep earlier. But I hardly know her, really. She's an elderly person, not well, and it's dark and cold. . . .

Let's call Eric first, in our own house.

When he's answered, I hear the music being played for you.

"A lady's just arrived," he says. "Catherine . . ."

He also says it's inspiring to be with you.

I feel rich and proud — like a host from a distance.

My address book is a mess, so for the mailing of the cards, I ask him to bring all the papers from the drawer of my desk. There are private ones he's not supposed to read; once more this is something intimate I'm learning to share. And I'm learning to be happy about it.

Your appearances as a dancing, running girl and an Egyptian priestess or princess are still very much with me, and toward midnight, a text for the mourning card comes to me: *In contrast with our car accident, the peace and sublimity in which Marian died are a profound consolation.*

Sunday, December 27th

During the night I've had to ask for strong painkillers a couple of times. What on earth is wrong with my back? I have to concentrate on each inch of each movement. The bedside table is really too far away and too full when I reach for things on it. Moving is time-consuming and exhausting. I've been impatient, and a muscle imposes punishment. I must focus on the serenity around you.

Resting above a tea-light candle is a bowl of water with rosemary oil. The scents of roses, candles, and the oil are a balm. The chain of love is never interrupted. The watchers make tea or coffee for each other — everybody is at home with you, while you are also with us.

After breakfast and washing up, I go to the children with Ernest and Nicky. We take a tray full of paper, envelopes, pens, and addresses, and settle by the girls' beds to do the work together. I've dreaded this task because the names and numbers in my address lists are in chaos. Last year you bought me a beautiful address book. It's been sitting and waiting in the middle of my desk.

The helpfulness and quietness of Ernest and Nicky have healing effects. Phoebe plays silently with her latest presents (a puzzle, a building kit), and Rosemyn colors envelopes in an awkward position on her back. "This is Mam's soul. . . ." Lovely streaks in pastel shades.

It's hard work, but at noon a few piles are finished, and we're thoroughly pleased.

Unexpectedly, your father comes in. Phoebe looks up, and her smile grows as broad as her face. She's missed him for ages; he's so much like you! She doesn't say anything, just goes on playing, maybe thinking: *Mam will be here any minute now.*

Again and again comes the question of whether I'll go to the funeral or at least say good-bye to you at home. Many are sorry that neither your parents nor I know how special it is to be with you.

They suggest that I take a wheelchair taxi and go in peace and privacy tonight. That's a good idea. I'll wait to see whether I'll be able to go — my last chance: I could be with you one more time!

Ann calls. After some fear and reluctance, the four of them have decided to fill a gap in the vigil tonight, so that all our neighbors will take part, even if they're no more used to this than I am.

Wearing earplugs, I'm trying to sleep for an hour. But I also want to think of a cherished object for you to take on your way, and some of the mail Jack has brought from home can't wait either.

Now the printer is here to collect the text for the mourning card. Size and layout are to be so different from the usual that I'm worried about the result, wondering if he's understood my ideas.

Timmons interrupts and insists on one point: *Written condolences only.* And I'll be grateful for that.

At all hours of the day I remember somebody I've almost forgotten to notify. Some are so close or live so nearby that they're not in our address books. And others: I'm not sure if you'd send them word.

Meanwhile, all the earthly fuss in which big and small matters alternate, the difference between them fading, is both cruel and pleasant — as a distraction:

What obituary must be sent to which newspaper?

Do the children get enough squeezed oranges?

Who will buy me slippers? The physical therapist gets mad when I walk in socks.

We need shampoo and picture books for the girls.

Is a phone book available here?

Should I buy a double grave? How does that work?

In between, I drink coffee with hot milk or fresh orange juice, made by countless volunteers.

Your funeral will be tomorrow at half past ten. Friends and families are to meet you at home, but how will that be arranged? I'm trying to think about the music. Your favorite tapes are there, but what live music would be possible? The piano is out of tune. Pat would play the flute, but she's close to childbirth and not well. . . .

Just when I'm giving up, the phone rings: it's Geraldine. She's back from the Ardennes and would like to be with you later this afternoon. It's strange: I forgot to worry about that part of the schedule. Then she asks, "Have you thought about music for tomorrow?" And before I've recovered from yet another "coincidence," she goes on: "Do you know what I've been singing these past few days? 'A Flower Is Springing.' Shall I sing it for Marian?"

It's been three years since we talked about that so hypothetically. And so profoundly.

The flower in the original text of this carol is a *rose:* "Es ist ein Ros entsprungen."

You played Praetorius yourself.

I'd like to ask two brothers, two brothers-in-law, and two neighbors to be the bearers of your coffin. Unfortunately, Richard has a slipped disc. Six women have volunteered, but I'm afraid they underestimate the weight. In any case, Trish will take Richard's place. John has a bad elbow, but he insists on carrying you.

Timmons has disappointing news: when leaving the house, they'll have to put the coffin on a trolley because the hall is too narrow for bearers. Peculiar, how the practical side of life keeps interfering, seeing to it that we keep our feet on the ground.

It's become a habit to take my evening meals "upstairs" (by elevator, from the fifth to the sixth floor).

In Phoebe's hands a slice of bread looks as if it's been borrowed from giants. Her left eye is still half-shut, and she moves stiffly, seems to be falling all the time. She forgets in a minute what she or anyone else said.

Later she says she's frightened but can't tell of what.

I ask Rosemyn who is to read her poem at the funeral.

"Annicka," she says immediately.

After dinner I have to lie down (since the 25th, my guest bed has been left here), and it's obvious I'm unable to go to see you; there's nothing to be weighed or considered. I must be careful not to press beyond the limits of fatigue; as it is, I'm glad my temperature hasn't been taken for a few days.

I'll copy Rosemyn's lines neatly, because they will be her send-off gift to you. She's already checked several times to see if it's ready.

Phoebe wants you to take the little lavender doll that was under your pillow, and I've chosen the rose quartz you received for your last birthday. Jack and Trish will search the house again, because I can't remember where it is.

Anxiously I ask them to take the last hours of vigil early tomorrow. Jack is just glad for this opportunity to say good-bye. After returning from Highflow, they were shocked to hear you'll be buried tomorrow — so soon.

For the same reason, Trudy had to "save" two night hours for Annicka.

I ask her to find the music you listened to so often during the last weeks of your life. It ought to be played for you and for those who'll be there to see you off.

You had to take a stand against my anger about that mantra music. Now I realize that you knew its original purpose underneath the commercial version, like an unconscious awareness of what was about to happen.

And now I'm bewildered by the many preparations you made, as if you were urged on, working hard to leave the house behind the way you wanted it to be — for us. Which is also a paradox: you wouldn't go until it was finished.

When I phone a few old friends, it shows how strong a bond can be that hasn't been expressed for years. How to tell them we've been dealing with your death for two weeks now? They can't grasp that within a few minutes, but they'll be leaving for Southmere in the early hours. Work is canceled, baby-sitters are summoned — daily life put aside.

It's the middle of the night.

In turns, in the cold darkness, your beloved are heading for you, with whom *farewell* receives a new meaning. They're lost in thought, let memories come, breathe in the scented oil they used to burn with you, read in silence or out loud from a favorite book, check the candles, wash cups and saucers, pick up members of the doll families, choose new music, sing Tibetan songs. . . .

It's seven degrees below zero. Still, some get on their bikes to come over at two or four in the morning. Weeks later, I'll find out that I forgot to tell Jack about the heater; it's switched off automatically at eleven p.m. But I'll be reassured: even those who came to stay for two or three hours never grew cold at all! They simply won't believe the heating was off.

Monday, December 28th

Phoebe sleeps until five-thirty this morning. Again she is afraid but can't say of what.

She enjoys a bath, but sadly, her hair is washed as well.

Rosemyn wakes up too. It's a good thing they're together at a moment like this, even if Rose needs more sleep herself.

Rose was noisy and boisterous this morning: screaming, calling names . . . She's testing how far she can go. When I tell her so, she calms down.

Doesn't the nurse know her mam will be buried today? Or doesn't she know that some emotions may be expressed in a roundabout way? It's true, though: the fierceness of Rosemyn's reactions often annoys me too. And I'm the one who *knows* her — I think.

My nights begin to have a certain pattern now. At about three a.m. I just need to accept being helpless, ask for the right drugs, and tell myself: It's OK, you *won't* get addicted. Every morning they bend the rules and let me sleep late (until eight), and breakfast is a blessing — brought in just like that.

At eight, Jack is with you — the last one to keep vigil.

The sweater and skirt you're wearing, with the necklace of shells, make him think of a scene from Polanski's *Macbeth,* with the noblewomen in long, handmade gowns on the beach. What an image: nobility, simplicity, the coast and the Celtic element, where you felt at home.

With Cor, he moves furniture around to create more space in the room. They take all necessary initiatives and make the final preparations for your send-off.

Since it's early Monday morning, most stores are still closed, and I don't know what people do to get flowers in the middle of winter. Still, they're brought in large quantities: roses, lilies, daisies, freesias, daffodils, carnations, branches of berries and wild greens arranged into lively bunches. . . .

Phoebe is sitting up in bed, doing a jigsaw puzzle.

Rosemyn is having trouble eating and drinking.

At nine-thirty I go up to their room with my candles and the most special postcards received these past several days — for you, about you. I arrange them on the bedside tables. A nurse fetches four glass holders for the candles. From the wall I take the painting of roses that Elisa made for her cousins and put it among the cards.

After ten o'clock, I tell them as much as I can about what's taking place around you.

The living room and kitchen are crowded. Nearly everyone is on time, including those who left during rush hour to make the long drive. Some of them have never been to the new address before; did I give them directions for this labyrinth of estates?

There are few seats, but a number of women absolutely need to sit down. Hopefully they're looking after themselves.

There's no "program." Who will speak? Who decides when?

Ernest says an introductory prayer. Then Mam explains modestly, "I've asked Arno if I could say a few words." And she renders how she sees the essence of your life.

Genesis 5 is about the genealogical register of the patriarchs: a list of awesome men. Their age is mentioned and the number of sons they begot — two important matters for men in the ancient world. But about one of them something else is added that has always fascinated me: "Enoch walked with God."

What's it like, to be walking with God? I've often tried to discern that in people, but it's not easy. Until I got to know Marian better: she is walking with God!

It would be hard to give specific examples. Her whole being was pervaded with her contact with the Eternal. She was not one of those who profess their faith on Sunday morning and then return to the order of the day. She opened her mind to the Eternal on *all* days, and that could clearly be felt. If the kitchen sink was full of dishes and the floor was covered by toys and jumble, that would hardly be noticed in the atmosphere of harmony, of which Marian was the heart.

She invested a great deal of herself and her views in

the children. She had only six and nine years to do that. Marian was no saint: she had her flaws, and from time to time there was a lot of trouble to cope with, but she walked on and got the strength to do it. That's the wonderful thing about walking with the Eternal: when you stumble, you're lifted up to watch the endlessness of a higher world, to be stronger on your feet afterwards.

In the course of the years, Marian told me, "Without suffering, we can't develop fully on our ways to eternity."

Marian is still walking with God, which can only be thought of in images now, like a ship at sea, getting smaller and smaller until it's gone from the horizon. It does sail on, and you know it's there, but hidden from our eyes.

Alex reads a poem by Ida Gerhardt, the double meaning of which touches something in me that has scarcely existed so far.

We are walking together,
the Father and the child. . . .

Annicka takes a piece of paper from your coffin and reads "I Am a Child of the Light," which is how many have seen you these days. They know how you tried. And the light has shown that you've succeeded.

It is silent.

These people in our own house are sharing something that's raised above earthly emotions: nothing seems to be ponderous. Differences in backgrounds of belief can fall away in the pureness and closeness of this farewell.

After one wrong start, the a capella, four-voice "A Flower Is Springing" sounds like crystal, so clear, both strong and vulnerable.

Finally, the silence deepens for one of the moments I find the most difficult, because we don't know yet how you'll be *staying* with us, how you will always be at home here.

Lauren lays the poems, the doll, the gem, and drawings by several children in the coffin; then John fastens the screws of the lid.

I know it's only your body that is shut off like this forever, but I still think of it as *you*.

It turns out that you can be *carried* outside after all, with one strong bearer in front and one behind. And that's a great comfort, even if it seems to be just a small detail.

Today's weather is clear, the sky very light.

Alongside the path is a tight row of people.

Everybody will find their way to Gorsemere separately, but Dad insists on driving right behind you, saying, "We won't leave her alone for one single moment."

In the cemetery, many more people are waiting, called and invited spontaneously by anyone who deemed it the right thing to do. They form a circle around you again.

Dad speaks. "Now that we hand Marian over, we commit her to the Eternal's trust, who is the source of all life and the remembrance of names."

Trudy reads the hymn about Light and Purpose.

(Mam remembered you chose that for our wedding service.)

Annicka reads Rose's poem.

Their voices are frail in the frost.

Most eyes are on you — all attention is completely focused — but Geraldine and Jerome are watching the light above the treetops. It's still a pure and beautiful place, where woods and open land meet, where you rambled a lifetime ago. And they see twelve swans, flying over this very spot at this very minute. (Jerome is a bird expert, and the swan sanctuary is nearby; otherwise I wouldn't have believed them.)

An escort of honor?

You've come through twelve days of pain and waiting.

Someone will tell me that December 13th is called St. Lucia's Day, the celebration of light. There are twelve days between that and Christmas.

The coffin is lowered.

Judy gives one loud cry in the silence, like a primal scream of mourning on behalf of us all.

For now, Elisabeth is the only one who throws earth on the coffin.

Without any kind of hesitation or introduction, Rosemyn mutters,

"I am dead
I am heaven
I am the earth."

And after a time of contemplation, the three of us each lost in thought, united beyond the words, she goes on.

"Light
grass
God
water."

It's like the four elements we seem to be enveloped in — softly, firmly, warmly. Is God the Fire of Love?

In the cemetery hall, there's coffee with cake and, as one always hears about such gatherings, a certain happiness or even cheerfulness, which inevitably comes with a profound sort of satisfaction or relief after an intense experience like that.

Strikingly, many return to your grave and throw earth on the coffin. The little thuds are finishing sounds, making things real and definitive. So *after* coffee, another circle is formed of its own accord. Some have never met before, but today they're a family.

Thea: *We go on living in your spirit, or in any case we'll make you live on through us.*

We've listened to Monteverdi's *Vespers* again. When people come and hug us, we can feel the coldness and freshness of the air on their cheeks, of the outer world braved for us and then shared here, where the contrast between cold and warm seems to dissolve.

Nicky fetches my meal from 5 West. I listen to various accounts of the morning, and an uncle or aunt helps our girls eat their lunch. A new era has begun, while yours does not end but will be relived.

I'm given the cards that came with the flowers for you. They're not addressed to me at all, and their intimacy, even of the traditional *rest peacefully* in shy handwriting, shows the extent of your friendships.

With gratefulness for everything you shared.

And from Muriel, the scribbles of a seven-year-old: *Bye, Marian.*

To her mother she said, "At Marian's, I could *always* stay and play."

At the end of the afternoon, Judy's here with her family, with lollies and chocolate bars for Rose and Phe.

"Your dad will be mad," Judy says, winking defiantly at me.

And they're so pleased with the candy, as if they've starved for weeks!

The four kids play games and work on puzzles. I must have watched them, overwhelmed by their ease and their ability to be engrossed like that. Or I was numb, sedated, lost, because I can't remember *what* I did or felt.

Gradually everybody goes home, and I'm taken back to 512. Only Rosemyn and Phoebe stay where they are.

I always draw the curtains early, so I'll hear about the

sky much later: a vast part of it is bright red for the first time this winter, and high above, the moon is joined by one big star.

Tuesday, December 29th

My first shower takes about half a morning. There's ample space in the bathroom, with a special chair, and on the walls are solid bars to hold on to.

Meanwhile, my room's cleaned as well, and even the bed is like new.

Someone from Home Care comes to talk about *afterwards,* that very new phase — to come much later. Do we have to go home again? I'm fine here.

We're on a list to receive forty hours of Family Care a week.

We're still a family.

But what if Phe and I can leave sooner than Rose? She's moving too much; I'm sure we'll be told again that the fracture hasn't healed properly. . . .

When we were putting the mourning cards into the envelopes, she wanted to help. I was afraid of smudges and creases, but Dad sat beside her on the bed and steered her movements just like a pal, until a nurse came in and gave her a warning.

I write a "notice" and put it on the head of her bed: *Dear visitors, please help R lie still.*

Her friends go ice-skating. In the middle of this Christmas vacation, the weather is ideal for spending long, careless hours on the ice outdoors. Parents come to watch, join in, wipe wet noses, pull sleds, give a hug after a fall, smile about a near-fall, bring gloves and lunches with hot cocoa.

The south view from the girls' room has an unreal beauty: sheer sunlight in rimed space. Each visitor brings in a tingle of frost.

Although it freezes hard by day too, Joan staunchly comes by bike with her lyre (she spent the little money she had on the instrument rather than a car). After the frosty ride, tuning the lyre is difficult. I'm there only once to hear the music, which is so ethereal that I'm afraid to move. The memory of her playing in the ICU has faded.

Phoebe starts asking about home. She knows you won't be there, but her rabbit will!

She enjoys working on puzzles and being read to.

When she mentions your death, she always says, "What a shame."

Rosemyn keeps a copy of the mourning card in a drawer of her bedside table. The staff haven't got a copy yet, and to Janet, who hasn't specifically asked for one, she says, "Do you want to see Mam's card? My poem is on it."

When Janet takes it from the drawer, she can also see a sheet of paper full of wild, black scratches.

"Mam's really dead," Rosemyn says emphatically.

Janet has the Christmas holidays off, but she had an inexplicable urge to go and get something from the ward (which she'd never done before on her days off) and pop in to see Rosemyn — just like that.

Today I bring the medicines from home to 6 East — one of my first new tasks — but Rosemyn reacts vehemently. "I don't need them anymore. That's over."

Perhaps because she used to get them from you.

Nurse's report: *She really lives for the mail, and when that's late, she gets mad.*

In the mail, from a colleague who is celebrating her fiftieth birthday in Paris, acutely aware of the contrast with your situation:

Dear Marian,
in Nôtre Dame,
the rose window
has all shades of blue
that look so good on you. . . .

From the mail I also learn the following. Herman was invited to your funeral. I hadn't thought of him, but somebody else had. Did you know that his wife got killed in a car crash when she was pregnant with Milly?

132

He found it hard to tell Milly about you, and first he said, "I need to go to a funeral."

"OK, so somebody's dead. Who?"

"Remember Rosemyn and Phoebe?"

"Sure."

"Their mother, Marian, has died."

For a second, Milly was silent. Then she asked, "And their father? Is he alive?"

"Yes."

"Then it's all right."

Lauren, Alex, and Phyllis are taking a walk in the forest. There's no wind, no motion. The land is still uniformly white with the rime. It's a normal Tuesday afternoon, but in this stillness they encounter two peacocks. It tests their sense of reality, because the animals are just as white and quiet as their surroundings, and one of them has its plumage fanned wide open.

Wednesday, December 30th

Rosemyn has slept through the night, but her arm is hanging wrong in the traction device because of her turning and twisting.

X-rays are taken, and my fears are confirmed: she'll have to stay in traction for a bit longer. So we need to surrender — it must be for the best — and we're painfully tough.

Phoebe's been out of bed a few times, to walk around or play at the little table. Beyond the bathroom is the world, where she once was.

She's always hungry and thirsty. With this open, pure look in her eyes, she says every minute, "I've got thirsty."

"Later, Phe."

I gather it's one of the clinical symptoms of her injury: no sense of limitation.

And just as often she'll be nodding, "OK."

Then again, "Give! Can I eat that? I like that. . . ."

"Later, Phe."

When the dietary assistant asks her, "What would you like to drink with your meal?" she says, "Oh, just fries."

Her body may be on earth, but she doesn't always know how to deal with it. "Can I wake up after sleeping?"

Rosemyn asks one of the nurses, "When can we go home?"

"Oh, maybe next week."

"How many nights is a week?" Phoebe asks.

"Seven."

"Oh, then we go home in seven nights."

I can wheel myself to 6 East. It's amazing how deft one can get with a chair like this; again, I feel like I'm in a movie. But I quickly learn that I'd better consider the muscles and nerves connected to my healing ribs when dealing with the elevator doors and especially with the heavy swinging doors that keep children from leaving the pediatric ward. A slamming of one of these doors has already cost me a night's sleep. From now on I'll call for someone to open them beforehand.

The physical therapist teaches me how to walk with crutches. The first couple of days I'm not allowed to practice on my own, and I don't insist, because when I'm not worn out from the exertion, I go up to see the girls or take care of a dozen other pressing matters.

I've decided never to take any kind of physical risk again. Late at night, I do vacillate between bathroom and bedpan and may take the walker as far as the door. But I stay on the safe side and return to bed — to be humble and use bedpan or bottle.

Since I'm "walking," it's really time for slippers too.

"I've bought these crazy ones," Phyllis says.

They have Indian patterns (that's not the crazy part) on fake velvet lined with orange synthetic material. It's humorous, but not exactly what I had in mind. How much courage do I have for honesty these days?

Depends, maybe, on how important it is.

"Do you want me to return them?" Phyllis asks. "I've got the receipt. Those 'real' moccasins they had were the wrong size."

But being dependent on so much help and effort and humor, I'm not that brave yet. Let's wear them right away, on a trip to the bathroom, and lo and behold . . . I'll never suffer from cold feet again!

Sitting on the toilet, I study them closely, differently, and all of a sudden I can see it: they're *father* slippers! More like grandfather's, one might argue, but fine, sure, I'll start with an outside detail and work my way inward.

Rosemyn and Phoebe love them, keep touching them to feel how warm and soft they are.

The mail brings a special moment every day. The very greeting in a letter can prompt deep feeling:

"Dear good Arno . . ."

"Ah, Arno . . ."

Some people write to Rosemyn and tell her they've actually looked into heaven, "to see a new, beautiful, and unforgettable angel. . . ."

Some write only to say that they're unable to put their feelings into words.

And I'm particularly moved to read how someone's memories of you are kept alive, sometimes from before I knew you, like the way you nibbled at a cookie during homework: it lasted an hour.

The neurologist comes and sits by my bed, taking his time. He observes me thoroughly and asks, "What would it be like if Phoebe and you could leave before Rosemyn?"

After the shock, I feel like embracing him, because his eyes tell me that he understands my anxiety about this and that he'll be able to arrange something which will allow us to coordinate our discharge.

I don't know what causes it, but after Joe and Erica have arrived, Rosemyn has an outburst.

"Why did you look back?" she yells at me.

"Are you talking about the crash?"

"Yes!"

"You mean I looked over my shoulder?"

"Yes!"

"I don't remember anything. But when you drive, you do that often, for all sorts of reasons. . . ."

She looks at Joe. He nods and says, "It's done without thinking — all the time!"

"But not when there's a *bend*," Rosemyn shouts.

"No. I saw that bend too late."

"So it's your fault!"

"It was a very stupid thing to do. Sometimes it's happened before you can help it. I didn't do it on purpose; it happened *to* us. What if you or Phe asked me a question. . . . Or you were fooling around. . . ."

"Or you were making jokes. . . ."

"Right, that goes on in all families, even in the dark and even before a bend. Still, few accidents happen. You may call it horribly stupid or cruel, and I'm responsible, but no one is to blame."

We look at each other so deeply that tears come to our eyes. Joe and Erica are silent. Phoebe is doing a puzzle.

"OK?" I check.

Rose sucks her thumb. Then she lets me comfort her. In the wheelchair I can't put an arm around her, so I get to my feet and lean on her bed.

When I leave, Phoebe is half-asleep. In the doorway I call out again. "Good night. . . ." And then Rosemyn says, "Can I wish Mam good night too?"

"Of course. I'd like that."

"Will you too?"

"Yes. Inside."

"Will we meet then?"

"That would be great, wouldn't it?"

"Me too," Phe mumbles under the blanket.

Back in 512, I need some support myself. Joe has come along, and we try telling each other that something only takes place in a certain way because that's how it's *supposed* to go; otherwise, it would happen differently.

He says that many people have been to the scene of the crash, wondering in dismay and disbelief how the car could have been drawn straight to that lone big tree, all that way, just missing smaller obstacles (by an inch) that would have stopped it sooner and less violently, or at least have changed its course. As a scene in a macabre movie, this wouldn't be taken seriously.

Rosemyn asks Erica to read from *Little House in the Big Woods,* and she doubles over laughing about a funny fragment she must have heard so often before.

I don't wish you good night until eleven p.m. At this hour I'm often too tired to focus on you properly, but now I remember the girls' plan.

I'm not asleep yet, just very "empty," concentrating on

breathing, and suddenly, in this openness, we're together at home. You're sitting on my lap at the dining table, wearing your golden brown outfit. I can't see your face; your arm is around me, and you're bending close to me. It's an image of fatigue but also fulfillment — we're comrades.

Well, that was no picnic, but it's done.

The soberness is significant, a result of *your* energy. I don't do anything; I'm not in the clouds. Actually I'm quite conscious of being in the hospital at the same time — receiving what you want me to feel.

Thank you for the confirmation and encouragement. How characteristic of you to meet me once more, fusing our worlds. I'll really take over what you began.

"Hold on by letting go" is a line from the mail.

Again I presume this must be the last contact we'll have across physical borders, to fuse heaven and earth in such a way that we'll be able to go on, all four of us.

Forever I'll feel the three times of your presence:

Dancing in the fields: freedom.

Learning an important task: concentration.

Coming to me in the dining room: satisfaction.

Our ways and directions are clear, even if it will be a while before I've reached your point of departure.

Thursday, December 31st

It's New Year's Eve in no-man's-land. You are there and you're not; we've buried you but mourning hasn't started yet; we're talking about going home although I'm ready for a rest; I'd like to be alone but need some company as well.

My temperature is taken as we go along, and it's 100.5. I go to sleep too late, let visitors stay too long, make too many phone calls. What if I come down with something that will complicate the situation even more, forcing me to appeal to all these people again. . . .

Many now have the headache, the backache, or the flu for which there was no time during the past weeks. Circumstances demand time for reflection. Some go away for a few days.

"Six more nights," Phoebe declares, and when she sees my hesitation, "The nurse said so."

Perched on her teacher's lap, she sings all the school songs. What a relief that such a large part of "before" has remained intact.

When Phoebe finds peace and quiet — when she's alone with one person, for example — she begins talking about you of her own accord. "I have to tell you something very sorry."

While Phyllis is reading to her, Phe says, "That's what my mam always does. Not anymore. She's dead now. So sad. Dad says that she wanted to die, but I didn't want it."

"Neither did I," says Phyllis. "But sometimes things happen even if you don't want them to."

Phoebe looks relieved, realizing it wasn't her responsibility.

She spends hours at the little table in the room without demanding attention. But, moving her stiff neck, she carefully follows everything that's going on around her. She refuses to leave the room without Rosemyn.

Even on New Year's Eve, Trudy is here, and Phoebe tells her, "The rabbits must go inside, or else they'll die from the fireworks." We didn't have the rabbits last year, but she knows the bangs will terrify them to death. In her own way, she seems to be remembering more than ever.

Trudy phones Cor, and he puts the two hutches on top of each other in the shed. Beats me how he's managed that; it was already crammed full.

Early in the evening I try to take a nap in order to be "fit" for midnight.

Lauren, Alex, and Phyllis come for a drink, and the hospital offers us sodas, cakes, and hot snacks. Too bad we're not very hungry.

For a short while I'm alone before Mam and Dad arrive. It's good to lie still and muse with closed eyes. In the daytime there's still too much going on for me to take it all in at once — no time for contemplation. I mean, for grief.

At midnight it's unpleasant to wake the girls from their deep, healing sleep, but I promised! Mam and Dad and I are the only "visitors" allowed here at this hour, which has a poignant side to it as well. It takes a great deal of effort to wake Phoebe. Afterwards I'm glad, though, because the girls' bliss is a source of inspiration, saving me from other sorrows.

The Happy New Year wishes — among the five of us — seem to sound awfully normal.

To get the best view of the fireworks, we can go to the other side of the wing. With Rosemyn in bed and Phoebe on my lap, we ride through the cold, ghost-lit corridors.

There happens to be a heavy fog, but at the height of this floor we get some light patches, and what we *can* make out we admire intensely. Three times over, Phe says, "This is the prettiest I've ever seen."

We have cakes and soda; then fatigue and melancholy get the better of me.

Back in their room, Rose and Phe go to sleep, fully content.

This would make a nice conclusion: you and me lingering in the doorway before going to bed ourselves.

Mam and Dad take me back to 5 West and then have to drive home fifteen miles — past "the scene." The fog has grown so thick now that sometimes visibility is nil. For part of the way they're forced to drive at a walker's pace.

Friday to Sunday, January 1st to January 3rd

For a brief time you're completely gone. I even have trouble seeing your eyes or hearing your voice. Perhaps I have to plunge into my new life now.

That keeps going in two directions at the same time: we're planning for our discharge from the hospital, which will be an ending of something that won't be truly lived until afterwards.

With each step I take on crutches, so many new and necessary possibilities arise that joy is mingled with courage and despair.

By chance, during visiting hours, I end up in an elevator, sitting in my wheelchair and bathrobe amid normal people in nice clothes. Ah, right, the outer world. . . . I can see their glances — "What's *he* got?" — and I seem to be an old, ugly, odd case.

All over the world it's a festive day.

At ten a.m. friends arrive who didn't get home until three in the morning, after driving through the fog, having to stop now and then to find out where they were. But here they are, cheerful and all, bringing a painting and a poem that were done years ago but are about you and now:

Heaven and earth unite,
twice am I. . . .

When I phone Lauren, it takes a long time before she can genuinely wish me a happy New Year. I don't think many of these routine wishes are felt as keenly as this one.

It's crucial that we be happy.

To what extent your happiness is still influenced by ours, I don't know, but it helps to be thinking that way.

The wound on the side of my leg is no longer dressed. In the shower I let the bandage slip off. I've never looked at the cut itself.

Taking a shower remains a tricky affair (I secretly skip every other day). One time the rubber cap on one of the crutch legs comes off, and the aluminum leg finds no footing on the tiles, making it impossible for me to move. Very consciously, I think: What if . . . While usually I'm quite stoic: What could possibly happen to me?

I need to call loudly for help, like a kid. This is the first time I haven't locked the door! They would have dealt with a locked door as well, but I'm wet, naked, thin, and cold enough without a crowd watching me.

The staff call me "mobile" and "virtually independent." At the idea of a nearing independence at home, I'm bewildered by my fear of failure, but maybe that's a case of self-pity or theatricality — which I'm *not* going to give in to.

The stiffness of Phoebe's neck looks rather bad. When she

turns her head to the right, her whole body still moves along with it. Some of the nurses are worried too. According to the neurologists, this will go away in time.

Her half-closed eye is also a tragic sight. Still, it's a miracle that this is the same Phoebe as the little creature of last week. So don't worry too soon! That would only impede her recovery. And she deserves to start anew and be whole again, doesn't she?

But that goes for *every* child!

She has headaches too, I think, but denies that for fear of more examinations.

From Phoebe, the staff learn that we're going home next Wednesday. A doctor has spoken to her.

Rosemyn has been picking at the wound on her eyelid, and some pus comes out. She'd better be on her feet soon. The traction is getting to be a disaster; we're growing more and more nervous about the next X-ray.

Phoebe has become so mobile that Rosemyn makes her tidy up and fetch all kinds of things. Sure enough, the nurses stand up for Phe, who for that matter makes it clear she won't be dictated to. But she does like neatness.

The fact that she walks around freely and can build a kit of Noah's Ark with visible pleasure must be a harsh blow to Rose — stuck in her cage. A hot, crunchy ham-and-cheese toast for lunch is some compensation. So sweet of Janet!

By now, Rose's long hair has turned into such a bird's nest that the nurses have basically given up brushing it. I admire those who've done that so far and survived Rose's shrieking and wailing. Shall I take her to the hairdresser's here at the hospital for a cute, roguish boy's cut? No, no, when I think about all the things you did with that hair . . .

In the void at the beginning of this year, you're here again after all, in various ways.

Suddenly your face appears, which was missing in the moment at the dining table. You're laughing, throwing your head back, like you did when I paid you a compliment: pleased, proud, shy, disbelieving. Again I'm quite awake and aware that this is not coming from me — too often I've tried in vain. It's you, almost physically present.

Annicka has needed days to recollect herself and cope with our conflict. She's watched a film called *Beaches* and now gives me the lyrics of Bette Midler's featured song: "It must have been cold there in my shadow. . . . Did you ever know that you're my hero? . . . You are the wind beneath my wings. . . ."

I don't know the movie and stupidly think that Annicka has written this for you — and that I should have written it myself.

Late at night, when my emotions have settled down, I phone to thank her and almost forget to say that I've found her gemstone again.

A gift from a colleague of mine:

> Far am I the outer,
> moving strong circle
> when from the heart
> all water is touched.

The deepest splashing
heaves in wider ripples
to the side — some reeds
are stirred: an angel goes.

When I closed my eyes,
they were opened slowly —
I saw the angel walking
and thought: like floating.

Monday and Tuesday, January 4th and 5th

Most people return to normal working days, which
wouldn't occur to me if I didn't have to make a visiting
schedule.

On that other Monday morning, Jack skipped work to
be here with Rosemyn.

Mothers and fathers are taking their children to
school. That was a real chore for us; you often went four
times a day and *always* in the early morning.

Your earthly love has been spent; you must truly be finding peace now. I only hope that you don't miss Rose and
Phe. There's so much to be missed about them. But there's

no such thing in the spiritual dimension — I've just told Rose that myself! I need to beware of projecting my own feelings onto you.

Phoebe has begun to say, "I need to cry a bit, you know," or, "I feel like crying."

Her grief comes when she sees the photo with the two of you roaming through our meadow filled with dandelion fluff, or when she thinks of her rabbit or has lost Annicka's gift, a little box with six tiny puppets from Nicaragua.

I can't keep count of all the presents she and Rose get, but they know exactly what is whose, although Phoebe never knows what to call the givers: "the woman with that name, and the little brother who was here yesterday . . ."

"Brother" may be friend or cousin. "Yesterday" ranges from last year to five minutes ago. And "the woman" may be a close friend.

In every possible place there are toys that form their world but are new to me. Twice a day I come from far away to admire something, play a game, peel an apple, and talk about you.

"Mam would love to see our children," Rosemyn says. "And she would take us to go late-night shopping."

"I can do that — soon."

"But we're so scared you'll die too."

"Don't think so. I've just been saved by a miracle."

"How?"

"I didn't have a seat belt on and fell out of the car, so I wasn't crushed."

"And why was Mam in her seat belt?"

"Well, you know what she was like. . . . She did everything the proper way."

"That's mean!"

"Yes. But I think Mam still would have died, even if she hadn't worn her seat belt."

"Why?"

"Her door didn't open, so she was caught in the car. Apparently, her work was finished here. She can rest now."

Rose puts her thumb in her mouth and stays angry.

Conrad says, "You didn't want me to take pictures during Marian's farewell. . . . Is that still how you feel about it?"

"Yes."

"Well. . . . You see, I did take some."

We give each other a searching look.

He worked in such a way that no one noticed.

"Rose and Phe may want to see them — one day," he says.

Suddenly it dawns on me that he's the one who knows what he's talking about — two years after Hanny's death — and I'm glad about the photos, even if I don't want to see them yet.

I notice how much can happen to me in a single day, how life is on the move and changes continually. Yet it needs to be lived moment by moment.

Conrad also tells me he saw a copy of *We're Not a Bit Scared* the other day — my first book for children! He opened it at random to the page where the mother has to slam on the brakes, and Mo flies around the car, landing comically on her head, because she wasn't wearing a seat belt. The "accident" ends well, and the mother goes a little crazy from relief, dancing in the street and crying, "We're alive! I braked on time! But we were terribly stupid; after this you will *always* put your seat belts on." And finally, "Come on, girls, let's go and tell Dad."

"About the seat belts?" Mo asks.

"No, goose, that we're alive!"

In another chapter, Mo has a concussion after a fall. When I read that passage to groups of children, they always laughed hard when Maggie shouts, "Don't lie there all crazy!" and, "Maa-aa-aam! Mo's dead!"

I didn't think of Hanny's brain tumor or of any other dying children until the book was out. Trudy and Conrad don't mind, they say, but can we make jokes about death? Kids do that on a daily basis. But would I write these funny stories now?

After eating a sandwich, I want to peel an orange and ask whose plate I can use — and find our old Phoebe again. "Take mine. Rose has finished too, but mine is cleaner."

I'm still scared to go up to their room on foot, unless there's someone who can bring the wheelchair along, which works a few times in the mornings. The hardest part is to stand in the hot elevator, and once on the way back Mam and I forgot to press my floor number on time, so that we descended slowly to the basement. My temperature is still over a hundred, but in the elevator it feels several degrees higher.

In my wing I do walk down the corridors by myself, going as far as to the stairwell, where I should be experimenting to see whether I'll be able to maneuver up and down the stairs at home.

On some walls of these corridors are large aerial photographs of nice scenery in the area. Close to my room there's a picture of Field Mansion, the site of our crash. After three weeks I discover this and stop in front of it. It takes me a while to orient myself to the captured view. Then I realize that the tree itself, past the driveway, is just outside the picture.

A dollhouse has been brought in for Phoebe; she seems to fit in it herself. By now, she dares to cross the corridor and go to the bathroom, and often she walks past Rosemyn to stand by the window and watch the world outside. Rose lies with her back toward that — or ought to be lying like that. But she squirms and turns to watch any details of the world beyond the glass. She looks for a star, even before it's quite visible in the dusk, and when a glint of the sun appears on the edge of a cloud, she says, "Just as if Mam is peeking around a corner."

Today, Rosemyn gets out of traction.

When the bandage is taken off — there's a deep wound on her elbow — she's impressively brave. Why is this done without my being there? Other ordeals have been endured without the presence of a parent, but this could have been arranged easily. It's my fault: I've never even *asked* about the procedure. And Rose doesn't mention it herself, either before or after.

This time they put her upright more gradually. She remembers the previous occasion very well, when she vomited, and her second confinement in traction has been much longer.

She's rather subdued, even shaken, they think. Suppose the bone still isn't healed? Is the surgeon having doubts too? Is that why she's not allowed to leave her bed yet?

Her reaction comes at six o'clock: a storm after the calm. She's so upset that it takes me fifteen minutes (though seemingly many more) to understand what she's talking about. The Advent calendar, which has been at the head of her bed from the beginning, is missing. Since today? Janet thinks it was gone ten days ago, when her first traction bed was returned and I hadn't even been to her room yet — when you were alive.

I remember something like that from her visits to me in bed, so horribly long ago. She shows me a snapshot of herself in traction, taken on the first day, her face covered with wounds; I can see the calendar. She's clutching the photo desperately.

Might it be tracked down somewhere in storage?

Janet promises to make inquiries after the bedtime rush (the ward is crowded with "cases" who could wait until after the holidays). But she'll find the calendar in their own room, in the "miscellaneous chest," filled to the brim with toys and presents.

When Jack comes to read to the girls, I'm glad I can return to my own quarters, where I ponder and realize what an Advent calendar means to Rosemyn: coming downstairs in the early morning and opening a picture in the delight of surprise, with you and Phe. On December 13th, twelve of the twenty-four miniature mysteries were revealed. I don't know if Rose opened any more herself on the remaining days, the twelve of your waiting.

During the night, Rosemyn throws up.

Early the next morning, she's taken to the X-ray department (without me) and later, when the surgeon comes with the results, we're afraid to look at him. What's the expression on his face: gloominess? But in a roundabout way (after saying there are still places here and there that need to heal), he tells us that Rose can stay out of traction. We can go home tomorrow or the day after.

That appears to be up to me. And part of me doesn't want to think about it. Tactfully, the surgeon hints that an extra day of rehabilitation is advisable for Rosemyn, and to my relief Phoebe reconciles herself to the fact that her careful count of the remaining days doesn't work out. "Day after tomorrow" is soon enough for her.

Rosemyn can have a bath! With a great deal of courage and patience and anti-tangle cream, a nurse manages to unravel the bird's nest in her hair. Rose bears it well and gets a present afterwards.

Looking like a fairy princess with her arm in a sling, she enters my room after a delay of two hundred and forty hours, saying, "I don't want to talk about Mam anymore, because that only makes me sad."

The neurologist comes to tell me that they'll do another EEG on Phoebe tomorrow.

Rosemyn has told him that I was looking over my shoulder at the moment of the crash, possibly, he suspects, because she'd asked me a question, and he advises me to bring this up (indirectly), because she may be troubled by feelings of guilt. His involvement is remarkable; Rosemyn isn't even his patient.

I act upon his advice immediately, but again it shows how hard it is with Rose to establish what is wish or fear and what is fact. The other day, after Leon had come with my mam and dad by car, she claimed with an authenticity that made me check her statement, "He went back by bus later, because he wanted to stay with me longer."

I don't achieve anything in my conversation with her. Can't she or won't she recall anything from the moments before the crash?

Wishing me good night, Phoebe says, "I must really cry."

"Because Mam is dead?" I ask.

"No. Something else . . . I'm scared. They have to do something. To me. A man who comes here said so."

"Oh, you mean the EEG. That's a kind of photo they're going to take. Just like the X-ray they've made of Rose's arm, remember? That's not scary, just a bit crazy. It happened before, when you were asleep, and you didn't notice. Do you want me to go with you?"

"Yes."

"No need to be scared anymore, then?"

"No."

We only share small parts of the days, and I can't catch up with the rest yet.

A lot of aspects of daily life are so *new* to Phoebe that they're frightening by definition. She has no idea what an EEG is, and I know it will be traumatic for her. If I picture her among those machines and unfamiliar nurses, I'm more worried than I've been so far. It could ruin the joy of our discharge.

My mind is trying to point out that I'm overreacting (after all, I'm overwrought, aren't I?), but I feel sure about this: Phe will have a rough time, which may do her more harm than good. And I'll have to leave her alone with the technicians.

Tonight I'm crying, not only about Phoebe but also because I'm dreading returning home without you. Up to now, I've just regarded that as something in the distant future that has nothing to do with me.

Rosemyn and Joe have to deal with a final shock. Joe has rubbed her cold feet and read to her, and in order to shift her in bed, to tuck her in nice and comfy, he takes her by the upper arms automatically, firmly. I've done the same thing. Seeing Rosemyn lying in bed now, it's easy to forget she's been in traction for three weeks. And one lifts a child by the arms all the time!

She screams. Joe wants to jump out of the window

from distress, but instead he informs the nurse, then stays until Rose falls asleep. He starts crying on his way home, calls the hospital again — everything's OK — and decides to phone me about it tomorrow. So brave.

Rosemyn can't have felt real pain; her arm has healed very well. I think she just had a psychological reaction to the newness of her arm being free and exposed.

The painter calls and asks if he can resume the job in our house. The thought takes some getting used to, but I'm actually delighted. Everything is being painted white. It will smell new. But isn't he reluctant to enter the house on his own, in the darkness of early morning, where a dead person stayed recently?

After a long hesitation, I want to ask Laura to phone our friends in France. I lack the courage and energy to write a letter or make a phone call in French, but the idea that they don't know anything about your death yet is beginning to haunt me.

Can I really ask someone to make a call to France with news like this?

I make a direct appeal to Laura. And guess what: she's already done it.

Some of the mail addressed to the three of us is in fact meant to be heard by you. Even those we didn't see very often miss your matter-of-course presence in a school-room (picking up the girls and helping out) or cycling along the river dike. They've all seen how you blended in with the land and felt how you gave so much by being yourself — some of which, as is so often the case, isn't valued enough until it's gone.

———— ✺ ————

Wednesday, January 6th

Phoebe has wet her bed. Have scientists discovered or admitted yet that it's a tension-related problem?

I arrive on time. A picture book is used to prepare children for an EEG, but the pictures don't exactly look reassuring to me. Rosemyn studies them eagerly. How would you tackle a situation like this?

Give Rose's curiosity a chance. Stay close to Phe, and don't be afraid yourself.

Via two elevators and many corridors, a transport assistant wheels her to a remote corner of the building. It takes all my strength and deftness to keep up with them in my wheelchair, and we only just fit in the elevator for patients' transport.

Hurrying along, I give Phe a smile, a wave, a wink. When I lag behind in a long corridor, she tries to smile back.

The nurses are sweet. Their brisk, nothing-to-worry-about manner makes us pretty nervous, but Phoebe gives polite answers to their questions. The gel they use is cold, and the points of the squirt tubes are sharpish and hard, but she's terrific about it, and I'm pleased she doesn't hide that it hurts.

Would she like to watch in the mirror and see how funny she looks?

No, thank you, that doesn't seem like a soothing idea.

Does she know this or that CD?

Some pop drone is played (a torment even to my *un-damaged* head): part of the examination or a diversionary technique? I suppose they don't know that we're all raw, sensory perception.

Then, when the shrill, science-fiction-like machines are switched on, I have to leave her alone.

"Back in a minute," I tell her.

She nods.

Out in the hall, I need to find some physical support first; then I try to be one with Phe inwardly. My mind is quick to find a distraction, but I strive to be *empty* of thoughts, wanting to be a channel of help for her, like the ultimate prayer: feeling divine guarding or reminding ourselves it's always there.

Coming out of the exam room, Phe's still frightened, but it went well, and they pay her big and honest compliments. We're very proud, and our pursuit race back to 6 East would rival a scene in a Hollywood movie. After a narrow escape from a monster, one can deal with anything.

The frost is over. Annicka and her sons come cycling through the rain, bringing a large, homemade Twelfth Night cake and a box of gemstones.

It's intriguing that twelve days before as well as twelve days after Christmas there are festive religious days, even if they've faded into minor or forgotten ones.

Three peas are hidden in the cake — playfully symbolic reminders of the Three Kings or the Wise Men? — and those who find a pea in their slice of cake may choose a gemstone. We're all together in the playroom, and like the mother of a big family, Annicka cuts fat slices for everyone.

But all kinds of toys and electronic games like table football are making noise, and it's wearing. Besides, Rosemyn's and Phoebe's things need to be gathered and packed; there won't be time to "move house" tomorrow.

The boys help: they take drawings down from the walls and roll them up, go to the staff room and ask for bags, borrow trolleys from 5 West. . . . The girls are busy sorting clothes, candy, music tapes (and retrieving the matching empty boxes), toys, games, books, dolls, presents. . . . Annicka is coaching them, and I coordinate the operation from a chair.

We feel incomplete, nervous, uprooted, and hypersensitive, but very excited.

Meanwhile, Trish and Ann have begun a huge cleaning job in our house (I never even needed to ask); the beds are remade, and not one speck of dust will be left anywhere.

Early in the evening, Rosemyn and Phoebe are horsing around. They've built a slide on one of the beds and are whizzing down, screaming, falling over with the giggles — a scene from a dated children's book that always ends well.

After Phoebe has settled down again (I've talked about home), she asks, "What kind of Mam do we get?"

"A lady from Home Care. She's very kind."

"What's her name?"

"Don't know yet. She's just like a nurse."

"Or like Karen and Rianne."

Her eyes are wide open with hope, innocence, and unawareness.

To Jack, Phoebe says, "What have you come for? Oh, I know, to read to us."

"No, to bring your shoes, for tomorrow."

So far, she's shuffled around in homey slippers here.

"Oh, my favorites!"

She strokes the furry edges and plants them by her bed so neatly beside each other: her first steps into the future are precise and characteristic again.

Trudy comes at bedtime on their last night in the hospital, the last of the nights that will never really be past.

I notice that one can grow attached even to crutches. The new pair from Home Care Services are different, and I have to start all over with them. It's so strange how we cling to familiar little things now. I part with "my own ones" wistfully.

Sometimes there's too much mail to cope with during the day. I keep a few letters for late at night, when I'm alone with you, to share a bit of timelessness.

Thursday, January 7th

From seven-thirty in the morning, it's a race on crutches: taking a shower, washing my hair, eating breakfast, getting dressed (two words for a moment that confuses all times and feelings: what's happened to my Peruvian sweater?). And then I'm taken for a checkup at the lung doctor's.

There's still a kind of stain showing on the X-ray, but he says that's harmless. He knows about my temperature and warns me about strain in such a caring way that I won't forget the look in his eyes.

Before Lauren and Elise arrive at ten (I asked Rosemyn who could take us home), I'm wrecked, but the excitement has restoring or at least diverting effects.

Fortunately, the nurses are used to saying good-bye. In the children's ward, they're all waving. It will be some time before I truly grasp what they've done for us. In my ward it goes even faster; it didn't occur to me that "my nurses" could be off duty or very busy elsewhere. Soon there will be someone else in my room.

What happened in this room seems to be lost.

We're in Lauren's car, and it strikes me that I don't feel anything peculiar. Nor do Rosemyn and Phoebe mention the last time they were in a Volvo with me.

It's only a five-minute drive home.

We go around the back, and I stay in the yard for a while. Where have you planted the bulbs? There were a hundred, weren't there. . . . With the girls. Just on time. Just a few weeks ago? I can see the satisfaction on your face, the pain in your back and soil on your hands.

Rosemyn is everywhere at the same time, except in our bedroom, I think.

Phoebe is with her rabbit, but it doesn't know her anymore and looks twice as big. Overwhelmed by its strong, brusque movements, she can't hold it — and her hand is scratched. She doesn't show it hurts, though, and I'm sure they will share life soon again.

Inside, it's warm with flowers, paintings, postcards, a thermos of coffee and cakes.

Lauren gives us yellow roses a bit shyly — knowing only too well what they bring about in me. I feel like crying, but that can wait.

The girls get "Four in a Row," the game they often played in the hospital.

Trudy brings four roses, one for you, and a postcard titled "Star of the Hero," which may surely be "Heroine."

On behalf of Baker Street, Annicka brings a beautiful

copy of *The Secret Garden*. How I'd love to be lost in that for an hour or so. But hours are whirling away.

Sitting on a chair at the dining table, I let life turn pages I haven't finished yet.

The phone keeps ringing.

I have to get up and sit down again so slowly that soon my knees feel like pulp.

At seven-thirty tonight, I go to bed, right after Rosemyn and Phoebe, climbing the stairs on bottom and hands. Mam follows with the crutches. I'm so glad I had a shower at 5 West this morning; how long can I skip that now? I brush my teeth, more or less, and say a quick good-night to the girls. It's impossible to stop and think how they feel. Here's the second flight of stairs.

Up in our room, I really need to cry, more with exhaustion — so it seems — than with grief. Mam starts crying too. Slightly embarrassed, we can't help but lean against each other.

She's afraid to leave me, but now I want to be alone, to lie down and surrender.

There's our bed, with the romantic quilt full of roses. And I'm longing for 512.

The present does not include me or you.

Suddenly I realize all kinds of things at once: my watch and my medications are downstairs; I have no water; Mam and Dad are leaving, locking the doors; Jack and Trish gave *their* keys to Lauren this morning; I can't sleep without a Seresta and painkillers; I'll get very thirsty and desperate to know the time, and I'm unable to deal with the stairs again.

Loneliness fades into a sense of responsibility: if Rose and Phe have nightmares, it'll take me ages to get there. And not until now do I think of the phone extension up here. To my surprise, it still works, and I call Jack, who can just intercept Mam and Dad (for the keys) in the car park.

He brings water, the pills, and my watch, and he keeps the keys so that I'll feel safe. But most of what he's brought is not definable.

I take your pillow and all the other cushions in the room to improvise something that should resemble my bed in the hospital.

I don't want to have a body anymore.

United in their V's, the geese are still flying over the fore-lands, toward a new patch to feed. At the window of our loft, it's just as if I can touch them in the slightest of nightglow.

Their cries are trying to remind me of you.

They needn't. Everything *is* you.